WHAT ARE THEY SAYING ABOUT Q?

What Are They Saying About Q?

BENEDICT VIVIANO, OP

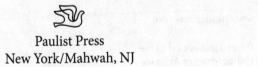

Paulist Press
New York/Mahwah, NJ

Cover design by Jim Brisson
Book design by Lynn Else

Library of Congress Cataloging-in-Publication Data

Viviano, Benedict.
    What are they saying about Q? / Benedict Viviano, O.P.
      pages cm
    Includes bibliographical references and index.
    ISBN 978-0-8091-4839-4 (alk. paper) — ISBN 978-1-58768-256-8
    1. Q hypothesis (Synoptics criticism) I. Title.
    BS2555.52.V58 2013
    226'.066—dc23

                                                           2012046219

ISBN: 978-0-8091-4839-4 (paperback)
ISBN: 978-1-58768-256-8 (e-book)

Published by Paulist Press
997 Macarthur Boulevard
Mahwah, New Jersey 07430

www.paulistpress.com

Printed and bound in the
United States of America

CONTENTS

Contents

PREFACE

This little book is intended as a brief introduction to past and present discussion of a hypothetical source for the sayings of the historical John the Baptist and of Jesus. It is hypothetical only as a separate document. It is not hypothetical in content. All the sayings are found in the canonical Gospels of Matthew and Luke, which are not hypothetical.

Readers may be curious about Q because it often comes up in discussions of the historical Jesus. Q is of value both for learning about Jesus, but also for learning about the Baptist, about the early believers in Galilee, and about how our later Gospels developed in part out of Q. Before or after reading this little introduction, the reader is advised to read the two hundred or two hundred and twenty verses of Q, whether found in a synopsis of the Gospels or in a separate edition, such as that by J. M. Robinson, *The Sayings of Jesus* (Minneapolis: Fortress, 2002). The actual text of Q comes to only thirty-five pages in that edition. The reader will be amazed at how early and authentic the verses seem (or "smell"— historical judgment being partly a matter of flair or "nose"). The verses also seem to form a coherent unity, despite some diversity of theme and language. The reader should ask: What impression of Jesus emerges from these verses? Are there any verses that seem inauthentic? What is missing in this picture?

In this little book you are now reading, at the end of chapters 2 through 5 there will be an example. This consists of a saying or paragraph from Q as reconstructed by modern scholars from the tradition common to Matthew and Luke. This quotation will be accompanied by a brief commentary. In two cases this will include a graph showing the relations between reconstructed Q and its later witnesses.

The literature on Q continues to grow. The present author does not pretend to have read it all. The bibliography at the end will lead the reader to longer and better books. The very existence of Q is debated. Some dismiss it as a figment of the scholarly imagination, as nonsense. Even among scholars who strongly support the existence of Q, there are debates as to its exact wording, its internal unity, its dating, and its central emphasis, whether it be a vision of God's future plan of salvation, or wisdom for living daily life, or a bit of both. Like anything, Q can be put to many purposes, some good, some bad.

The subject of this book interest any historically minded reader. It will especially appeal to readers who like Jesus, who are open to Jewish biblical styles of wisdom, or who are not afraid of ethical instruction or even of talk about a divine judgment. One can become a Q fundamentalist; however, the dangers of a fundamentalist approach will emerge clearly in what follows. This is a book that is "friendly" to Q, even enthusiastic, even if it does not absolutize the source, as one might who would say that Q represents the only true way to follow Jesus. Q represents a minimum program, not the whole of the Jesus tradition or of Christian faith. The point is that it offers a solid base, a good starting point for further exploration. The reader will be amazed at how rich even this short source is for learning about Jesus and the early gospel tradition.

I would like to thank W. D. Davies, Frans Neirynck, John Kloppenborg, and Dale Allison for all that I have learned from them, even if I have not always been faithful to their views.

Benedict Viviano, OP
February 16, 2012
Vienna

LIST OF ABBREVIATIONS

ABRL	Anchor Bible Reference Library
BETL	Bibliotheca Ephemeridum Theologicarum Lovaniensium
CBQ	*Catholic Biblical Quarterly*
ETL	Ephemericdes Theologicae Lovanienses
FZPT	Freiburger Zeitschrift fuer Philosophie und Theologie
JBL	*Journal of Biblical Literature*
JSNTSup	Journal for the Study of the New Testament Supplement Series
JTS	*Journal of Theological Studies*
NJBC	New Jerome Biblical Commentary
NovT	*Novum Testamentum*
NTAbh	Neutestamentliche Abhandlungen
NTOA	Novum Testamentum et Orbis Antiquus
NTS	*New Testament Studies*
PBC	Pontifical Biblical Commission

P. Oxy.	Oxyrhynchus Papyri
RB	*Revue Biblique*
RBL	*Review of Biblical Literature*
SBT	Studies in Biblical Theology
SNTSMS	Society for New Testament Studies Monograph Series
WUNT	Wissenschaftliche Untersuchungen zum Neuen Testament

1
INTRODUCTION

What Is Q?

The document called Q is a collection of 220 verses common to both Matthew and Luke but not found in Mark. It was noticed in the nineteenth century that these 220 verses bore a certain family resemblence. They are mostly sayings and teachings—and generally not parables, stories of miracles, or other events like the passion or resurrection of Jesus. They give the impression of being early, not showing much influence of post-Easter theological interests or themes. The nineteenth-century scholars suspected that these 220 verses were independently copied by Matthew and Luke from a source or collection of Jesus' sayings that as such is now lost. This lost source is what is called Q. The abbreviation Q is usually explained as deriving from the German expression *Logien-Quelle*, which means "Sayings Source." It could also be derived from the Latin word *quattuor*, meaning "four"; the sense would be that, besides the three Synoptic Gospels of Matthew, Mark, and Luke, there was a fourth source, Q.

The hypothesis of another early source for our knowledge of Jesus (and John the Baptist) presupposes another hypothesis, that Mark is the earliest of our four Gospels. This was concluded in the nineteenth century because of Mark's literary and theological roughness. In Mark, Jesus is regarded as crazy by his family, he

1

gets angry, his disciples do not understand, and there is little sense of a post-Easter church emerging. All this suggests an early place for Mark. Matthew and Luke tidy up and smooth out these rough edges. (This does not mean that Mark is as rough as he is sometimes taken to be. His narratives are very vivid and effective, especially his masterpiece, the passion narrative. Many have seen great literary cleverness and theological depth in Mark. But the fact that Matthew, Luke, and John have all felt the need to rewrite him, plus the late addition of Mark 16:9–20, the so-called longer ending, suggest that Mark is earliest.)

When Matthew, Mark, and Luke are laid out side by side, Matthew and Luke can be seen to be copying and reworking Mark at points. However, it also becomes visible that there are verses common to both Matthew and Luke that are not found in Mark. This is called the double tradition; this is what is called Q. So Q is a *corollary* of another hypothesis, *Marcan priority*, namely, that Mark is the first of the three Synoptic Gospels. The view that Mark is the earliest Gospel we possess as such, and that Q is the other early source, is called the *two-source hypothesis.*

One could stop here and say that this is just piling up one hypothesis upon another hypothesis. This is too fragile a way to proceed in gospel study, one might think. So another approach is to say we do not know the historical and literary relations between the four Gospels. Our picture of Jesus must then be a blurred one, with little critical assurance that one picture is better founded than another. We must be content with a sacred haze. However, this approach too builds on hypotheses. They cannot be avoided in science or in historical scholarship. The issue, rather, is this: Granted the inevitability of hypotheses, are the ones we choose prudent, reasonable, fruitful, helpful, and more precise than the alternatives?

Even opponents of Q nowadays usually accept the priority of Mark. Thus, the way is open for a theory to explain the material that remains common to Matthew and Luke and that is not found in Mark.

There are people who prefer a blurred picture of Jesus. Such a blurred picture leaves them free to construct or imagine their own idea of Jesus with greater freedom. The Q hypothesis, along with Marcan priority, is for people who may be compared to the woman with a hemorrhage or flow of blood in Mark 5:25–34 and parallels (Matt 9:20–22; Luke 8:43–48). She says in verse 28: "If I touch even his garments I shall be made well." She wants precision. In Matthew and Mark, she even grabs the fringe of his garment, the *zizit* in Hebrew. She wants a solution. So do two-source people. They want to get as close to the historical Jesus as they can, using their nineteenth-century methods.

Genre

Once we look at the Q verses as a whole, we see that they belong to a genre that is quite familiar to us: a collection of sayings or wise teachings. We can think of the Proverbs of Solomon, Qohelet (or Ecclesiastes), and Sirach in the Old Testament; the *Gospel of Thomas* among the early Christians (outside the New Testament canon); and *Pirqe Aboth* among the early rabbis. Such collections were quite common in antiquity[1] (as they are today, for example, the *Oxford Dictionary of Quotations*). But in this abundant and popular loose genre, there can be differences, with more or less structure.

The basic questions of introduction to the books of the Bible can be asked of Q: Who wrote it? When was it written? Where was it written? In what language was it written? Is the work we have complete (intact), or have parts been lost? The answers to most of these questions are in dispute among people who work with the Q hypothesis. Three different answers will be presented as part of the story of the history of Q studies in the rest of this book. But we can take a peek ahead now and say that the date of composition was probably before Mark's Gospel, which was completed between AD 66 and 75. That would put Q's composition between

the 40s and the early 60s of the first century. It was probably written in Galilee, and certainly in Roman Palestine. For a long time
people thought it was written in Aramaic. Now there is strong
support for it being written down originally in Greek. The collection is probably complete, but that is difficult to prove. A number
of additional verses in the Gospels could have belonged to Q. Usually the question of authorship is left unanswered as too speculative. At the end of this book we will try to suggest an author.

Q Summarized

Since this work does not include the entire text of Q, we
should give a little idea of its content and possible structure. (As
much as possible, we will follow the reconstruction of the International Q Project, without claiming that its decisions are absolute.)
Q begins with the preaching of John the Baptist, the baptism of
Jesus (possibly), the temptation of Jesus. Then follows Jesus' Great
Sermon (on the Mount or on the Plain, but no location is given in
Q, just the content). There are two passages about Jesus and healing, praise for John the Baptist, and statements about this generation in which Jesus identifies himself with the Son of man. Jesus
says he has no fixed residence, he demands prompt departure of
future disciples, and he encourages prayer for future workers/
missionaries. There follows another longer discourse, this one on
mission. This discourse ends in woes on unreceptive Galilean
towns and in the authorization of the disciples as accredited missionaries, as Jesus himself is sent by God. This authorization hints
at a high Christology or sense of Jesus' exalted self-consciousness.
This consciousness of being the absolute Son of the absolute
Father reaches a high point in Q 10:21–24, where we find a
thanksgiving for divine revelation, followed by Jesus' statement of
his filial consciousness, and then a beatitude or statement of con-
gratulation to those who have lived to see this day. Taken together,
these sayings form a powerful Christological package. (This is

true, but it is without the use of the terms *Christ* or *Messiah* or *Anointed One*. Those titles occur in Mark and Paul but not in Q.)

Then comes the Lord's Prayer and further teaching on prayer. This slides into a discussion of demon exorcism and from what source the exorcist draws his power. One must make a decision for or against Jesus (11:23). The sign that will be given is the sign of Jonah. Jonah is related to Jesus as the Son of man. Jesus is more than Solomon and Jonah (symbols of wisdom and prophecy, respectively). Then comes a list of woes addressed to Pharisees and lawyers. Personified wisdom judges this generation. The persecuted are exhorted to fearless courage and are promised the Son of man's heavenly support. But the Spirit is higher than the Son of man (12:10). Part of the discourse concerns true treasure and freedom from anxiety. The return of the Son of man coming in judgment is announced (12:39–46). Jesus presents himself as a preacher of fire, sword, and division (12:49, 51, 53). The crowd is encouraged to interpret the time (12:54–56). It is advised to settle out of court (12:58–59). The parables of the kingdom of God compare it to a mustard seed and to yeast in the dough (13:18–21; note the gender balance). The narrow door suggests the fewness of the elect (13:24–27). In the kingdom, fortunes will be reversed (13:29, 28, 30). Jesus laments over Jerusalem until his blessed return (13:34–35). Jesus praises humility (14:11). The parable of the banquet is told. The disciple must prefer Jesus to parents and to children. Disciples must take up their cross, risk loss of life, not lose their salty tang, and prefer God to Mammon. There is a salvation historical statement on the law and prophets in relation to the Baptist, and the subsequent violence to the kingdom of God. The law is eternal. Divorce is forbidden, children are not to be abused. The lost sheep are to be especially cherished and rejoiced over when they are found. The woman who finds her lost coin rejoices and we with her. (This parable is found in Luke only, 15:8–10, but Robinson includes it in Q because of the gender balance.) Forgiveness is to be practiced without limit. Faith is powerful enough to move a tree. Q concludes with a last-judgment or end-time discourse: The Son of man will come like lightning; the shock will be as in the days of Noah; some will be taken, others will be left behind; one must use one's allotted gifts (parable); the elect will judge the twelve tribes of Israel.

Problems Posed by the Contents of Q

The reader can see that the contents of Q are quite disparate. Scholars of the caliber of Martin Hengel have concluded that Q cannot be a unified document.[2] There are many efforts to overcome this dispersion of material in Q, and they will be discussed in later chapters. But we can already note that although Q is usually presented as a collection of sayings—without stories, parables, miracles, or a passion-resurrection narrative—in fact, it contains a bit of all of these smaller genres, except the passion story. It is also unified by certain themes that are trademarks of Jesus and the earliest traditions about him: the use of the term *Son of man* as a theological title, and the term *kingdom of God*. These both can be made into confusing puzzles by modern scholarship, but they can also be easily clarified against the background of the apocalyptic theology of the Book of Daniel. They come together decisively in Daniel 7:13–14. This passage is very probably the key background of Jesus' own thinking and preaching, as well as the key background of Q, of Mark, of Matthew and Luke, our earliest witnesses to Jesus.

More troublesome for the modern reader, used to relaxed democratic pluralism, is the content of some of the sayings in Q. The sayings on discipleship, family, "this generation," the Pharisees, and lawyers seem harsh. So it is well to remember that Q (and the Jesus of Q) is not for the faint of heart. This Jesus is not simply a nice, kindly rabbi, or a Galilean nature boy traipsing through the flowered fields in springtime. This Jesus has a unique self-consciousness and a sense of mission from God, and he forms disciples to follow in his difficult path.

   The three-part temptation story is so out of character for Q that at first blush most modern critics place it as a late addition to the sayings. This may be correct, but there are other solutions than simply saying it is late. The temptation story is mysterious, no matter who first told it. One interpretation is that the story is a midrash on three ways of not loving God enough, with heart, soul, and strength (Deut 6:5).[3] As such, it is a commentary on a text of central value to Jesus and to the synagogue liturgy. Strictly speaking, Jesus could have told the story himself, since he is good at telling parables and teaches the love command. In that case, it could have been collected from Jesus by Q and then taken over by Matthew and Luke. The view that the story is a midrash does not mean that Jesus was never tempted. It is antecedently probable, indeed certain, that he was tempted (think of Gethsemane!). But a temptation is usually a private, personal, inner experience. One can choose to tell about it in imaginative narrative forms. No one knows who first composed the story, but there is no need to place it in the last phase of the composition of Q.

   Since Q has at least a few clusters of material—the Great Sermon, the Mission Discourse, and the Judgment of This Generation—it is more unified than, say, the *Gospel of Thomas*, which is just one saying after another. But even in *Thomas* there are little dialogues between Jesus and the disciples, for example, *logia* 12, 13, and 114. Even though there may be no miracle stories in Q (in the reconstructed Q, Jesus is not actually said to have healed the boy), there is no doubt that Jesus is connected with demon exorcisms by his discussing them, even if it is not related that he performed them.

   Another point the reader may puzzle over is that Q contains both wisdom teaching and apocalyptic judgment preaching. Some scholars find these two genres, indeed mentalities, incompatible. But human existence consists of both life and death, sweet and sour. Ancient authors, like Daniel and Enoch, not to mention the Mishnah, hold them together. It is probable that Jesus, and thus Q, did too.

One of the most delicate questions concerns whether we should actually call Q a gospel, rather than only a source or document or collection; a hypothesis or a corollary; a preacher's handbook or a disciple's notebook. There is no rule in this matter. One is free to do what one wants. But Helmut Koester and J. M. Robinson have helped us understand the dynamics of gospel writing in relation to theologies and to different types of Christian communities.[4] They conclude by saying that only a gospel that contains the Easter kerygma (that is, the confession of the saving significance of the death and resurrection of Jesus Christ, such as we find in the creeds of the church) can found a church or be the basis of a church, a community open in principle to everyone (and, in that sense, *catholic*, meaning "universal"). That is why the church's four canonical Gospels, whatever their different accents, all have the passion, death, and resurrection story at the end. However, Koester and Robinson also recognize that there were a number of apocryphal gospels in circulation among early Christians. They group them into four types: words of the wise (like Q or the *Gospel of Thomas*); collections of miracle stories (like the *Protoevangelium of James*); apocalyptic books (like the *Apocalypse of Peter*); and passion-resurrection books (like the *Gospel of Peter*). Our four canonical Gospels contain all four of these early gospel types, but they all conclude with the story of the death and resurrection, and that is what makes them books of the church.

Before concluding whether Q is a gospel, we need to mention what I will call good and bad uses of Q. Q is centered on a different kerygma or religious message than Mark. It is centered on the coming of the kingdom of God in its fullness, brought by the Son of man. In modern theologies of hope and liberation, this brings with it a message of social justice and peace. On the other hand, Mark's message of the Easter kerygma is forgiveness of sins through faith in the atoning death of Christ and his life-giving resurrection. Now if for some reason you do not like this second kerygma, you can play Q's kingdom kerygma against it, since Q has no passion narrative.[5] This is a possible option. But it is not necessary, since even the classic creeds hold both kerygmas together: "He will come again in glory [that means, with the kingdom in its fullness] to judge [that is, to govern] the living and the dead. And of his kingdom there will be no end" (Nicene Creed). So there is no need to choose one kerygma to the exclusion of the other. One is free to place the accent where one will, within the larger framework. That is the option we will recommend. So, to respect the traditional primacy of the Easter kerygma, and to avoid abuse, we will not call Q a gospel, even though its message and kerygma are precious and should once again become part of the central message of the canonical Gospels.

2
THE DISCOVERY AND RECEPTION OF Q IN GERMANY

The story of Q begins in early Christianity and then leaps into early nineteenth-century Germany. It begins with Papias (ca. AD 60–130), who was bishop of Hierapolis in Asia Minor and was counted among the Apostolic Fathers. (Hierapolis, mentioned in Colossians 4:13, lay near Laodicea and Colossae; today it is the city of Pamukkale in southwestern Turkey.) Papias claimed to have learned from the oral tradition of the disciples of the Lord. His main work is preserved only in fragments quoted by Irenaeus and Eusebius. Papias gives us valuable information on Mark, and one famous sentence on Matthew. (He knew both Gospels.) Many Church Fathers then copied his remarks. Eusebius presented him as foolish; however, this was not because Papias was ignorant about what he reported, but because he believed in a literal second coming of Christ to earth to reign for a thousand years (see Rev 20:1–10). So Eusebius's low view of Papias was due to a theological disagreement, not to special information on his "historical value."

The First Mention of Q?

Papias's famous sentence on Matthew is this:

Matthew collected therefore in the Hebrew language [*hebraidi dialekto*] the sayings [*ta logia*] [of Jesus] and everyone interpreted [*hermeneusen*] them as best he was able.[1]

This sentence has provoked lively discussion at least since the eighteenth century, as people have asked about the authorship, place, and date of our four Gospels and about their possible mutual interdependence. Who copied from whom? This last question gave rise to a branch of New Testament study called source criticism. The question of which Gospel influenced the others became acute when, thanks to new printing technology, people could print "Gospel synopses," where the four are printed in parallel columns so that their similarities in detail and their differences could be seen at a single glance (*synopsis* in Greek). The first such synopsis edition was by J. J. Griesbach in 1778.

The "normal" use of Papias's famous sentence interprets it as saying that Matthew the apostle was the first evangelist; he wrote his Gospel substantially as we have it in Aramaic; others translated it into Greek. It has taken some struggle to disentangle the interpretation of this sentence. For one thing, the Greek word *logion* (plural, *logia*) usually means "oracle," a communication from the gods, although it can mean "saying," too. Still, if Papias had wanted to speak about a collection of sayings, it would have been clearer if he had written *logoi* (the plural of *logos*, "word," "saying"), rather than *logia*. On the other hand, since he was speaking about the sayings of Jesus, he may have reverently regarded them as divine oracles and deliberately written *logia*.

Another point of struggle is the phrase "in the Hebrew language." Almost automatically this is changed into Aramaic by modern translations. But now scholars are beginning to realize that the phrase could mean "in a Hebrew style." The Greek word Papias uses is *dialektos*, not *glossa*. *Glossa*, literally "tongue," means "language" in Greek. But the word *dialektos* can mean either "language" or "style." So Papias could mean: Matthew wrote in a Semitic-flavored Greek.

A third point of contention is the word *interpreted* (*hermeneusen*). This could mean that others translated Matthew's Hebrew into Greek, or that they wrote commentaries interpreting Matthew's work. If Matthew indeed wrote the *logia* in Greek, the second sense of *hermeneusen* (he commented on, or explained) is more likely.

Schleiermacher

Our story of the discovery of Q must now fast forward to Berlin in 1832. The theological star of the recently founded university there (1809) was F. D. E. Schleiermacher (1768–1834). He has been called the prince of Protestant theology in the nineteenth century. He is often denounced as a gaseous Romantic, who rewrote the Christian faith as if by moonlight. He made the faith to be all about uplifting feelings, and not about hard dogmatic truth. But this denunciation is not the whole story. He was a hard-working pastor and preacher who was also interested in understanding the four Gospels. He wrote his own life of Christ and a commentary on Luke, as well as hours-long sermons for each Sunday.

A few years before his death in 1834, Schleiermacher wrote a long essay "on the witness of Papias about our two first gospels."[2] In this essay, Schleiermacher carefully studies the Papias fragments to arrive at two conclusions. The first is the more important for us and will be presented in greater extent. From Papias, Schleiermacher gets the idea that Matthew the apostle had written down a series of *speeches* spoken by Jesus. Then he studies Matthew and sees the five main discourses that each end with the same formula. These discourses are the Sermon on the Mount (Matt 5–7); the Missionary Discourse (Matt 10); the Parables of the Kingdom (Matt 13); the Community Discourse (Matt 18); and the End of the Age Discourse (Matt 23–25). Since Schleiermacher is discovering this for the first time, he expresses himself in a more hesitant way than is being presented here, but the five discourses are there in his essay. He was a pioneer and groping his way. (In America we are used to thinking of the five discourses as being a discovery of B. W. Bacon of Yale University, but Schleiermacher saw the structure long before.)[3] Then Schleiermacher sees more teaching material scattered throughout Matthew. For him, all this was referred to by Papias. By the time he is finished, Schleiermacher has most of our Greek Gospel of Matthew as being accounted for by Papias's sentence.

Schleiermacher's second main point is that when Papias says that Mark was Peter's *hermeneutes*, this means that Peter preached in Aramaic or in such poor Greek that Mark had to *translate* for him into relatively clear Greek. For a long time, Papias's statement has been taken to mean that Mark wrote down the gist of Peter's preaching and storytelling, perhaps shortly after Peter's death in 64, that is, that he served as Peter's secretary, not primarily as his translator. It is only pertinent to our concern to note that Schleiermacher takes the Greek verb *hermeneuo* in one sense when he is dealing with Matthew and in another way when dealing with Mark. In the one case, it means to comment on; in the other case, it means to translate. Schleiermacher did not feel the difficulty as much as we do. *Hermeneuo* can mean both, but would an author have changed the meaning so abruptly in the same passage?

It is sometimes said that Schleiermacher is the inventor of the Q hypothesis. This is not quite true. He rightly saw that Matthew consists in part of discourse material and that this material plays an important part in his Gospel. But he did not see the possibility of the double tradition, common to Matthew and Luke and absent from Mark, as being derived from an earlier source of mostly sayings material, what we call Q. Like Papias, Schleiermacher neglected Luke. But in his ruminations on Papias's notice, he was coming close.

Strauss, Weisse, and Holtzmann

The year after the death of Schleiermacher, a bombshell fell on the playground of the theologians. A bold, young scholar in Tübingen named David Friedrich Strauss published a long life of Jesus (1835–36) that assumed the then-normal view that Matthew was the first evangelist. Strauss noted the supernatural elements (for example, the heavenly voice at the baptism, the view of all the kingdoms of the world from a high mountain during the temptation, the bodily transfiguration) and declared that they were myths. Strauss's book was quickly translated into English by the woman novelist George Eliot, and into French by the lexicographer Emile Littre. The book, still in print, provoked outrage. Many tried to refute it. In any case, it gave a stimulus to biblical studies.

An idealist philosopher from Leipzig, Christian Hermann Weisse (1801–66) was drawn to the stir and wrote a two-volume work on the gospel history (1838). To refute Strauss, Weisse sensed that scholars must get behind Matthew to earlier and simpler sources. He made three points that would be determinative for the story we are telling: He first judged that Mark was the written Greek Gospel on which Matthew and Luke depended. He then saw the double tradition of sayings common to Matthew and Luke; that is, he overcame the neglect of Luke. Finally, he concluded that Luke and Matthew each used the same collection of sayings, but independently of each other. These three points eventually became pillars of the two-source hypothesis.

A quick evaluation of these three points would not be out of place here. The first point, Marcan priority, has become a commonplace of biblical scholarship. The second point, that there is a double tradition, is a fact hard to deny. But that Luke did not know Matthew, that he wrote independently of Matthew, has come in for a lot of criticism. We could call it the weakest link in the argument. Let us anticipate a little. If one wrestles with the earliest gospel traditions, like the Marcan-Q overlaps or Luke's presentation of the sayings in the double tradition, it is hard to convince oneself that Luke had Matthew's version in front of him; that is, Luke probably did *not* have Matthew in front of him. To this extent, Weisse's third pillar stands solid. But this also entails that Luke was writing around the same time as Matthew, that is, between AD 75 and 95. Quite recent commentaries put both Matthew and Luke in that period. If, however, the view prevails that Luke wrote in AD 120, then it is hard to imagine that he had not heard of Matthew or seen his Gospel. Abstractly one could still argue that he knew Matthew but chose not to use him but rather Q when it came to the double tradition. Still, the whole edifice seems to totter for historical purposes. Therefore, it seems that those who accept the classic two-source hypothesis must struggle to maintain a medium date for Luke, neither very early, nor very late, close to the time of Matthew, but independent of Matthew. This is a burden and a risk.

It took some time for the value of Weisse's insights to be appreciated. He was not a member of the biblical scholars' guild, even though he was eventually asked to teach in the theology department at Leipzig. But by 1863, a textbook writer named Heinrich Julius Holtzmann (1832–1910) produced a study of the Synoptic Gospels wherein he gave a detailed comparison of the sayings in Matthew and Luke.[4] This was so convincing that the idea of Q or a sayings document gained general acceptance, a position it has held till today. Holtzmann's textbook was widely used, but was somewhat congested. His Q was embedded in a book that dealt with many other subjects. In this sense, his Q was not fully visible.

Von Harnack

That was to change when, in 1907, Adolf von Harnack (1851–1930) published his stand-alone edition of Q, in which the Greek text of the double-tradition parallels in Matthew and Luke were printed side by side, with commentary and notes on each set of parallels. The book was immediately translated into English.[5] This work put Q on the map, as John Kloppenborg says. It made Q a tangible, visible reality that one could study for its own sake. Soon Q began to be mentioned in books on the growth of the gospel tradition, and put into diagrams of development alongside Mark, but before Matthew, Luke and John, as though it were a manuscript and this were a matter of textual criticism.

Who was Harnack? What authority did he have? It can be safely said that Harnack was the most important German Protestant of the second half of the nineteenth century, indeed, up until the First World War, although he began to lose his credibility during the war, as we shall see. He began as a professor in rural Giessen. There he produced his *History of Dogma.* This was his greatest work, but not his most popular. That was an easy-to-read set of lectures published in 1900 titled *What Is Christianity?*— which filled the railroad stations of Berlin with cases of copies to be shipped all over the world.

Harnack's *History of Dogma* had caused some controversy. In it he defended the bold thesis that, with Luther, the whole idea of theological dogma had been abolished. This was made more concrete when he told students that when they became pastors they should not recite the Apostles' Creed with the people on Sunday. The German emperor, Kaiser Wilhelm, wanted to appoint him professor at the flagship university of Berlin. But the Berlin Church Synod refused to pay Harnack's salary. The Kaiser found a way around this by employing him as a royal librarian. Harnack's support from the emperor meant that, when the Kaiser and Germany were in trouble after the first months of the war, he was asked to write a statement that Germany's war aims were noble and cultural. Harnack was already president of the Prussian Academy of Sciences. His statement was signed by about 250 professors of German universities, including a few Catholics. But younger non-German theologians who had studied with Harnack were disappointed, even disgusted. They broke with Harnack and his brand of liberal Protestantism, which, they felt, had lost its capacity for a prophetic criticism of the prevailing culture and government policy.

Harnack was always putting his foot in his mouth, and he also tended to exaggerate. Although he claimed that there was no more dogma, Protestant churches were still defined by the twin doctrines of justification by faith alone and of the authority of Scripture alone. These functioned as defining dogmas in fact, no matter what label they bore. In addition, the Apostles' Creed came back into use in parishes when the people and the pastors wanted an identity badge against Hitler after 1933. But Harnack's edition of Q was a landmark. In it he defended a fairly high Christology on the basis of Matthew 11:25–27 // Luke 10:21–22, which he declared were authentic words of Jesus (which we will quote and discuss at the end of this chapter; but for now, let us hear Harnack's judgment on it):

> The transition from the designations of Teacher and Prophet to that of the future Messiah demands, both in the self-consciousness of Jesus and also in outward expression, some middle term, and it is difficult to see why tradition must be supposed to be in error when it presents us here with the designation "the Son."[6]

So, despite what he had said about no dogma in his youth, years later he was now saying that the road to Nicaea, the church's dogma, was still open.[7]

Archaeological support of the reality of Q was the publication of the first volume of the Oxyrynchus Papyri by B. P. Grenfell and A. S. Hunt in 1897. The papyri had been found in Upper Egypt. The first set of fragments that they published were claimed to be *logoi* of the living Jesus. When more of the text was discovered years later, scholars came to realize that the papyri were the opening of the *Gospel of Thomas*. *Thomas*, as we have already said, is a gospel that contains only sayings. The discovery was not of Q itself but only of a type of early Christian writing that resembles Q. Still, it helped to secure the probability of Q.

Siegfried Schulz

German Protestant interest in Q declined in the 1920s and 1930s of the twentieth century, although the two-source hypothesis continued to be the normal view of Synoptic Gospel relations. After the Second World War, interest revived. Siegfried Schulz (1927–2000), a professor in Zurich, tried to take up where Harnack had left off. In 1972, he published a little paperback with the Greek and German texts of Q, and also a large commentary book on each saying.[8] This became for a time the standard work in German. After an introduction on Q research, Schulz grouped the material into sixty-six sayings "units" and proceeded to analyze them. He was interested in the tradition history of the sayings.

He then divided the sixty-six sayings units into two groups. He thought that the first group of fifteen units provided the tradition or preaching of the Jewish-Christian Q community on the borderland between Palestine and Syria. It contained features like beatitudes and woes, the Lord's Prayer, prohibitions of revenge and of divorce, the love of enemies, the Golden Rule, warnings against collecting earthly treasures and judging others, warnings against useless anxiety and unnecessary fear, and encouragement of asking God for one's needs in prayer. Schulz thought that this first group of sayings reflected the post-Easter, charismatic, end-time enthusiasm that could accept a radicalized Torah observance and was full of the prophetic awareness of the nearness of the God of Creation.

The second group consisted of fifty-one sayings units. This group provided the preaching of the later Q community dwelling in Syria. It covered topics like the earthly Jesus, the delay of the second coming of Jesus in glory, the judgment on Israel, the bring-

ing back home of the lost sheep, tax collectors and sinners, discipleship to Jesus, and the community of disciples.

Schulz had thus roughly divided the Q material into two piles:
one was apocalyptic, was dated early, and was "good" (that is, with
historical value, due to its eschatological freshness); the other was
sapiential, or composed of wisdom sayings, was dated later, and was
"less good" (that is, with less historical value because it was "less
fresh"). This was his boldest move and led to a troublesome debate.
The next generation of scholars would turn this evaluation on its
head. They would say that the wisdom material was early and good,
whereas the apocalyptic material was later and bad. Both such
efforts are misguided. There is no necessary opposition between
wisdom material and apocalyptic material. Both types—apocalyptic, end-time judgment threats, and ethical instruction—are found
in the same books, for example, in Daniel, *Enoch*, and the separate
Gospels. One should concede that sayings collections, as such, are
an instructional *genre*, but should also recognize that this genre
does not determine the content in such a precise way that apocalyptic must always be included or excluded. Sonnets are a very pre-
cisely defined genre; sayings collections are not.

In Schulz's first group, the sayings show signs of charismatic
enthusiasm and prophetic awareness of the God of Creation. His
criteria for selecting them, when examined soberly, seem quite
arbitrary. They smack of early nineteenth-century Romanticism
(Wordsworth's daffodils), theological prejudice (prophecy good,
priestly bad), and Max Weber's conservative sociology (charism
versus routine). Weber's categories are used to this day to analyze
political candidates, so as concept formation they have enjoyed
great success. Whether they are useful categories to analyze the
dating of gospel sayings is less obvious.

Another area of confusion is the matter of Q and apocalyptic. The discussion of this issue is bedeviled by ideological
prejudices. Julius Wellhausen could be said to have developed
Germany's prejudice against apocalyptic on the grounds that it
was a late development in the literature of the Old Testament.

Apocalyptic only began with the Book of Daniel and with sections of Isaiah that were all written after the return from exile, and hence belonged to what Wellhausen called Judaism, as opposed to ancient Israel. The preexilic prophets had dealt with real politics. The apocalyptic writers were dealing in political fantasy; therefore, from Wellhausen's point of view, they represented a decline. In Wellhausen's his own day and place, the apocalyptic viewpoint was represented by the Pietists, distrusted by the state as not loyal enough.[9] The same dislike of apocalyptic was present in the English-speaking world. Anglicans dreaded the calculations of the end-time by the Plymouth Brethren. These calculations were judged a threat to their tidy church-state relations. A similar distaste was found in the United States toward Adventists, Mormons, and Jehovah's Witnesses. More refined distaste is found in the view that the *Parousia* in Q is negative because it involves judgment. It is true that the *Parousia* involves judgment, but this judgment includes judgment to salvation *and* damnation. This thinking in binary opposites is distasteful to politically correct moderns, but in the ancient circles that nourished these hopes and expectations, the accent was rather on salvation, the kingdom of justice and peace, the resurrection, and a correction of the injustices suffered by the poor and the righteous in times of oppression and persecution.

Given this confusion, it will be useful to state clearly the viewpoint adopted in this work of evaluation. For Q (and presumably for Jesus), the theological vocabulary of the kingdom of God and the Son of man derives from the Book of Daniel, mediated also by the community that produced the Dead Sea Scrolls found at Qumran, and also by John the Baptist. The Book of Daniel is the basis, and Daniel includes a theology of history based on four world empires that succeed one another in time and culminate in the kingdom of God and his people. This kingdom includes justice, peace, and joy. So it is basically positive in intent, even if it implies the defeat of the enemies of the people of God. The Son of man in Daniel is a heavenly figure who stands next to God and receives divine authority; in effect he is a divine figure. Thus, this title has what can be broadly called Christological implications, even if it does not involve the actual title *Christ*, which is not found in Q.

Text Study: Q on Christology

Let us consider an example of an important text: Luke/ Q 10:21–22 (// Matt 11:25–27). This reads in Robinson's reconstruction:

> At [that time] he said: "I praise you, Father, Lord of heaven and earth, for you hid these things from sages and the learned, and disclosed them to children. Yes, Father, for that is what it has pleased you to do. Everything has been entrusted to me by my Father, and no one knows the Son except the Father, nor does anyone know the Father except the Son, and to whomever the Son chooses to reveal him."

The reader will here be confronted with some hard decisions to make, and will see the promise and perhaps the disappointment of Q research in a most acute manner.

Taken together, the two verses Q 10:21–22 form a powerful text of religious revelation. In addition, the verses are united by the terms *Father* (five times) and *reveal* (twice), and by the contrast of *Father* and *Son*, explicit in verse 22, implicit in verse 21b. If they were spoken on the same occasion by the same speaker, namely, the historical Jesus, they would solve many historical problems in the history of early Christianity: They provide a basis, however slender, in Jesus' own thought and speech for the high opinion of him held by his followers. They provide a historical basis for the Christology of the Fourth Gospel.

On the other hand, one could drive a wedge *between* the two

verses and say that they represent two different micro-genres:
Verse 21 is thanksgiving-praise (Hebrew *todah*). Verse 22 fits no
well-known literary category, as it is a statement of revelation, religious knowledge. One could then say that because the two verses
are of two different literary genres, they are two separate sayings,
spoken (or written) at different times, perhaps decades apart,
meaning it is inconceivable that Jesus could have said verse 22.
Among more radical critics, it has become common to say that
Jesus spoke verse 21, so that it is authentic, whereas verse 22 was
composed after Easter by someone other than Jesus in the early
church. The close connections between the two verses (the repeti-
tion of *Father*, *reveal*, the implicit contrast between *Father* and
Son) can be explained by saying that verse 22 is a late, post-Easter
commentary on verse 21.

Against this view, one can argue that from the beginning the
two verses have formed a unity that they derive from Jesus. Since
the nineteenth century, one has seen the same structure in
Matthew 11:25–30; thus, verses 25 and 26 are thanksgiving for
revelation; verse 27, the content of the revelation; verses 28 to 30,
the great invitation to accept the revelation. A parallel structure
has also been found in Sirach 51. (Critics say that Sirach 51 was
not an original unity. True, but once the elements had been placed
one after the other in Sirach, one could read the chapter as a revelation in those three parts.) The contents of Q 10:21–22 are closely
connected by the themes Father, revelation, and Father-son contrast. In Luke, Q 10:21–22 are followed by the equally appropriate
verses 23 to 24: "Blessed are the eyes that see what you see! For I
tell you: Many prophets and kings wanted to see what you see, but
never saw it, and to hear what you hear, but never heard it." These
are Q verses (Matt 13:16–17). They flow perfectly from the pre-
ceding in both Q and Luke.

The reader must decide whether the slide from one micro-
genre to another necessarily entails different dates and authors or
not. To say yes involves according an almost magical power to genres. Granted the close relations in content between verses 21 and 22,

TEXT STUDY: Q ON CHRISTOLOGY

Q 10:21–22 (after Robinson)

²¹ At [that time] he said: I praise you, *Father*, Lord of heaven and earth, for you hid these things from sages and the learned, and disclosed them to children. Yes, *Father*, for that is what it has pleased you to do.

²² Everything has been entrusted to me by my *Father*, and no one knows the *Son* except the *Father*, nor does anyone know the *Son*, and to whomever the *Son* chooses to reveal him.

Matthew 11:25–27 (NRSV)

²⁵ At that time Jesus said, "I thank you, *Father*, Lord of heaven and earth, because you have hidden these things from the wise and the intelligent and have revealed them to infants; ²⁶ yes, *Father*, for such was your gracious will. ²⁷ All things have been handed over to me by my *Father*; and no one knows the *Son* except the *Father*, and no one knows the *Father* except the *Son* and anyone to whom the *Son* chooses to reveal him."

Luke 10:21–22 (NRSV)

²¹ At that same hour Jesus rejoiced in the Holy Spirit and said, "I thank you, *Father*, Lord of heaven and earth, because you have hidden these things from the wise and the intelligent and have revealed them to infants; yes, *Father*, for such was your gracious will. ²² All things have been handed over to me by my *Father*; and no one knows who the *Son* is except the *Father*, or who the *Father* is except the *Son* and anyone to whom the *Son* chooses to reveal him."

could not verse 22 be a bold second step by the speaker of 21? Is it conceivable that the earthly Jesus could think like this about himself? Or is this too bold? Is this a contradiction between Jesus as humble (Matt 11:29) and Jesus as the absolute Son of the absolute Father?

Let us try to answer some of these questions. From the point of view of Q studies, there is a Marcan-Q overlap of idiom. In Mark 13:32, Jesus says: "But of that day or that hour, no one knows, not even the angels in heaven, nor the Son, but only the Father." This saying, while embarrassing for a later high Christology because the Son confesses his own ignorance of something important, is usually viewed as authentic. It is not in Q as such. What is striking is the idiom: the absolute Son of the absolute Father. This is the idiom also found in Q 10:22. This overlap of idiom in two early independent sources supports the view that the historical Jesus could and indeed did think about his relationship to God the Father in this way, bold though it was.[10]

One finds a similar view of the compatibility of great humility and great claims in the Book of Numbers. In Numbers 12:3, Moses is the humblest of men (cf. Matt 11:28). Yet a few verses later, Number 12:6–8, God speaks with Moses mouth to mouth, a unique privilege (cf. Deut 34:10). Admittedly it is not Moses himself who so speaks. The Jewish scholar David Flusser has found statements of self-awareness by Hillel the Elder that resemble in their boldness the statements of Jesus.[11]

With the Q hypothesis, we can date Q 10:21–22 to AD 40 or 50. These verses belong to early Jesus material. This is the minimum payoff. The historian who judges that both verses go back to the earthly Jesus will not be acting imprudently. There are dogmatic or ideological prejudices at work on both sides of this judgment call. Earlier, we quoted Harnack's view that it goes back to Jesus. In his full discussion, Harnack makes it clear that it is for him only authentic when all "metaphysical" aspects of meaning have been removed. This is, however, more of an ideological postulate than a historical judgment. Ulrich Luz concedes: "That the saying originated with Jesus cannot be conclusively excluded."[12] Exegesis cannot force one to faith.

The purpose of this example has been to show how Q can help us make a reasonable case for one view over another. This example illustrates the fascination and value of the Q hypothesis. Theologically the verses provide the best Synoptic Gospel evidence that the "enlightenment view" is not adequately founded—that Jesus did not simply think of himself as a nice man, and that only after his crucifixion (and resurrection) did his greedy disciples invent out of whole cloth a higher self-consciousness for him. That the post-Easter church developed Christology further is not in doubt, but it is not obvious that Q 10:22 was designed as a commentary on Q 10:21.[13]

Excursus on the Possible Authenticity of Matthew 11:27

"All things have been given me by my Father [*Panta moi edothe hypo tou patros mou*]."—Matthew 11:27

"The history of its [v 27] interpretation has not yet been written."[14]

The interpretation of Matthew 11:27 and the judgment of its historicity have been bedeviled from early on by the crossing over of the main body of Christians from Semitic to Hellenistic thought categories. The Gnostics quickly exploited the verse to fit their anti-Jewish viewpoints. The Arians followed suit. The verse became mired in metaphysical disputes alien to Jesus and Q. The Hellenistic preoccupation could be summarized as *eternalism*, the concern that whatever is said of God must be eternally true. Only the eternal has value. Such a cultural presupposition has little place for revelation in history or for an apocalyptic worldview.

Early Christian Fathers like St. Irenaeus tried their very best to grasp this worldview, but they were still enmeshed in Hellenistic cultural categories imposed on them by the Gnostics and Arians.

As the verse became absorbed in the debates over the Trinity and Christology, the plausibility of its having been spoken by the historical Jesus receded ever further into the horizon. By the early twentieth century, it had become common in critical commentaries to deny the authenticity of the verse.[15] Only if the verse can be understood in Semitic, apocalyptic, and biblical terms—free from Greek metaphysics and the Hellenistic dread of time and history and change—does it stand a chance of actually having been spoken by Jesus, recorded by Q. We need an interpretation based on Jewish apocalyptic eschatology, if the verse is to be understood in its own cultural milieu. This eschatology includes Canaanite-Ugaritic cosmic combat myths as received in purified form by the Book of Daniel, the Book of Revelation, and by Jesus himself.

A Few Early Christian Interpretations of This Verse

The Gnostics **Ptolemy and Marcion** said that the phrase "No one knows the Father except the Son" means that the *known* God of Creation, the God of the Old Testament, is a different God from the *unknown* God, Father of Jesus Christ. Irenaeus tries to answer this. He overcomes the distinction between the known and the unknown God by appeals to Providence, to common sense, and to the preexistence of Jesus as divine Wisdom helping the Creation and knowing the Creator from all eternity. But the Gnostics also pressed the sense of the verb *edotha*: "all things *have been given* to me." The past tense (aorist passive in Greek) could imply that all things were given to Jesus *after* Creation and thus mean that he was not preexistent. If this were so, it would mean that for the Greeks he was not divine, because for them the gods are eternal and immortal; there never was a time when they did not exist. This is Greek eternalism. For Marcion, it was God the

Father of Jesus who gave him all things, not the God of the Old Testament.

For **Arius**, Jesus was created in time, and thus was not preexistent. So all things were given to him at his conception or incarnation or baptism or transfiguration or resurrection—but not from all eternity.

Against these views, the orthodox **Church Fathers** fought for one God who was both Creator and the Father of Jesus, and for the Son as preexisting from all eternity, not created. "All things *have been given* to me." But the gift could not be in time, and there could be no before and after. So the past tense of *edotha* was troubling to them. What sense could it have? They wanted a gift that always was and that always would be. They were prisoners of Greek eternalism. St Irenaeus refutes Marcion and the Gnostics by a Johannine interpretation of Matthew: The Son is the divine Logos in Creation and in continuing Providence, he is the permanent presence (*Parousia*) and the implanted Word.[16]

A Few Twentieth-Century Approaches to This Verse

Alfred Harnack saw the link of verse 27 with John and Nicaea. He saw its Q earliness and even its authenticity, but got lost in textual criticism. The verse goes back to Jesus but perhaps in a different form than the normal manuscript reading in our Greek New Testaments.

For **Julius Wellhausen**, the verse was an interpolation. *Panta* means "revealed knowledge." The verse is sapiential. This became the standard critical view.

Johannes Weiss was not very strong in his Matthew commentary. The verse is about Jesus' subjective feelings and is not from Jesus. Weiss's commentary smacks of nineteenth-century romantic idealism. But Weiss, in his epoch-making little book on the kingdom of God (1892), saw clearly the apocalyptic background of Jesus' preaching. The *panta* means the kingdom of God. Weiss did not, however, push his insight far enough. The kingdom theme in the Gospels derives primarily from the Book of Daniel, especially 7:13–14. There the kingdom is handed over to the Son of man, understood as a divine being. The divinity of the Son of man is now clear, thanks to the Ugaritic background (not yet available to Weiss). Jesus looked forward to the Son of man bringing the kingdom to earth (e.g., Mark 8:38), and he associated his own mission with that of the Son of man.[17] Q goes even further; it identifies the Son of man with Jesus.[18] Of course, Weiss could not know about Ugarit nor could he consult J. J. Collins's great commentary.[19]

Alfred Loisy, a French theologian who will be discussed later, attributed everything in Matthew 11:25–30 and Luke 10:21–24 to the early church ("*un prophete chretien*"), and nothing to Jesus. Denying that the verse was authentic was a typical approach for the times.

Our Own Proposal

The *panta* ("all things") should be understood as the kingdom of God, including the revelation of the divine plan for salvation history. This plan is often understood in terms of the seven eons of salvation history: from Adam to Noah, from Noah to Abraham, from Abraham to Moses, from Moses to David, from David to the exile, from the exile to Jesus, from Jesus to the Son of man returning in glory—who, for Christians, is identical with the risen Jesus Christ.[20] (There is a problem: in Mark 13:32 and its Matthean parallel, the Son has not received the full plan!) When Matthew writes the aorist passive *edotha* ("has been given"), this means that the Ancient of Days (God) gives the kingdom to the Son of man (Dan 7) *before* the incarnation of the Son but *after* Creation (at least of the angels); *after* the Son of man has defeated the Leviathan-Yam-Mavet-Lot-Lucifer (names for the leader of the forces of evil) in the cosmic combat (Rev 12). It is a time beyond time or mythic time. In medieval terms, it is "eveternity," the time of the angels. (The aorist passive could be perhaps taken as atemporal, though it is normally taken as snapshot past.)[21]

One can argue that the context of Matthew 11:25–26 and even the knowing in verse 27 require a sapiential sense. The *all things* means divine revelation. In the parallel Matthew 28:18–20, it is clear that the *all things* means the kingdom. In Matthew 11:25–30, there is a greater emphasis on knowing. This need not involve a rigid either-or. At the present time in Jesus' ministry, it is a question of divine election and human acknowledgment and obedience. So the mutual knowing is asymmetrical. At the end of the Gospel, it will be the kingdom that will be revealed or given.

In verse 27 there is reciprocity of knowing. There is also a certain exclusivity. No one knows except the Son and the Father. These claims are unprecedented. The verse is very bold. There is a partial parallel in Exodus 33:12–14: God knows Moses by name, and Moses asks to know God and his ways.[22] Jesus goes beyond this. He knows the Father. Jesus speaks somewhat like Lady Wisdom in Proverbs 8:21–31. But she is a personification of a religious value. Jesus is a historical person. It is obvious that such language is possible within the biblical tradition. No recourse to Hellenistic thought is required. But the total combination here is original, not necessarily redactional: Matthean, Lucan, or Q. The possibility, even the probability, of its origin in Jesus himself cannot be ruled out. There is a certain pride in verse 27, as there is great humility in verse 29; there is a parallel with the pride of Moses in Numbers 11:6–8 (although it is God who speaks so about Moses), and the great humility in Numbers 12:3.

That the Son should preexist is a Jewish (rabbinical, Talmudic) idea. (Strack-Billerbeck does not treat 11:27!) Based on Psalm 90, the Talmud lists seven things that were created before the world:

1. Law, Torah, future revelation
2. Repentance
3. Paradise (on earth?)

4. Hell (Gehenna)
5. The glorious throne (of God; cf Matt 19:28, Dan 7:9)
6. The (celestial?) Temple
7. The name of the Messiah

What concerns us here is the seventh of these items. That it is the *name* of the Messiah suggests that the name preexists in the mind of God the Creator and Redeemer, in a pre-personal, pre-incarnate, pre-historical way.[23]

The Talmud was written after Jesus, Q, and Matthew and Luke, but its idea about the preexistence of the name of the Messiah coheres well with the idea of the heavenly Son of man to whom is delivered the kingdom in Daniel 7. Jesus connected himself with the Son of man in his own mind and speech (Mark 8:38). This suggests that he thought that there was a divine element present with or in himself. But the moment when the kingdom would be delivered was not determined: conception, incarnation, baptism, transfiguration, or resurrection.

The point of these probes is to try to understand Matthew 11:27 in Jewish Palestinian terms, not in terms of Greek metaphysical theology; in terms that Jesus could and would have used, so far as we can discern from Q and Mark, our earliest sources about him, and from the datable contemporary sources, such as Qumran literature.

The point is not to claim that there is an unbridgeable chasm between Greek and Hebrew thinking.[24] The two cultures had been in contact since before Alexander the Great, 330 BC (1 Macc 1:1–8). But there is still a difference between Aristotle's *Physics* and his *Metaphysics* and the Books of Samuel and Kings. The difference is that the Greek works are characterized by a sober rational scientific approach, while the Hebrew books find meaning and a divine plan in and through the historical process, as well as in apocalyptic vision and hope.

The challenge is to make intelligible the cultural background of Matthew 11:25–27 within a Jewish salvation history and an

apocalyptic, eschatological context. With the aid of Danielic apocalyptic and biblical wisdom literature, this can be done. St. Irenaeus
was very strong on a millennialist apocalyptic eschatology in the
concluding chapters, the grand finale, of his *Adversus Haereses*,
but he did not use this approach when trying to deal with the
Marcionites' abuse of Matthew 11:25–30. He fell into their trap.
This has led modern scholars to think that if Irenaeus is right,
then the verse expresses itself in a cultural manner that is not that
of Jesus himself. If so, the verse is not authentic and the Christological problem remains historically insoluble, in the sense that
there is no basis in the historical Jesus for the later development.
This is antecedently improbable. If, however, we read the verse in
what is most probably its original cultural context, it could without historical implausibility be attributed to Jesus. The fact is that
Daniel does speak of a transcendental, heavenly divine being
alongside the Ancient of Days to whom is given all power and
kingdom. Jesus knew of this and thought in those terms. It cannot
be excluded that he thought of himself as the special son of the
heavenly Father, called to reveal the Father to others. That the
verse implies by its manner of speaking that Jesus has a strong
sense of himself (an ego) and that he had an element of will
(*choosing* to whom to reveal the Father) is clear. But these elements of ego and will are not historically implausible. Thus the
verse can reasonably be attributed to Jesus himself. This train of
considerations suggests the high adventure and the theological
promise of this approach to the contested verses.[25]

3
THE RECEPTION OF Q IN THE BRITISH ISLES

Although Britain had its biblical debunkers since at least Thomas Hobbes in the seventeenth century, its skeptics since David Hume in the eighteenth century, and its theological anti-trinitarians and philosophical radicals since the early nineteenth century, the Church of England on the whole stayed with a rather uncritical approach to the Bible until late in that century.[1] There was a powerful revival of doctrinal orthodoxy in the Oxford Movement, led by Anglican churchmen John Henry Newman (before his conversion to the Roman Catholic Church), Edward Pusey, and John Keble. The poet Coleridge tried to soften the doctrine of biblical inerrancy (*Aids to Reflection*, 1825). Broad church thinkers like Benjamin Jowett, in an essay collection called *Essays and Reviews* (1860), tried to shake things up in the established church in regard to the interpretation of Scripture. Jowett was driven away from theology and turned to philosophy and administration. But another essayist ended up as an archbishop of Canterbury.[2] Newman tried to rethink the doctrine of biblical inspiration but had to wait for Vatican II to be vindicated. The High Church Anglicans had to wait for Pusey to die (1882) for things to move. This occurred with the collection called *Lux Mundi* (1889), edited by Charles Gore, later bishop of Oxford. But after the First World War, there was a new spirit in the land to try to come to terms seriously with biblical scholarship and even to make a distinctively British contribution that involved an awareness of how societies actually work.

Streeter

This new era may be said to have begun with a remarkably readable book by Burnett Hillman Streeter called *The Four Gospels* (1924). Streeter (1874–1937), fellow of Queens College, Oxford, during the heyday of the British Empire, tried to take a global view of the issues posed by the Gospels (in 624 pages).[3] For him, the first issue was to have a reliable Greek text. So the first half of the book was devoted to textual criticism, the discernment of the best manuscripts, and their grouping into different families, which included a discussion of early Christian geography. Where were the centers that produced these manuscript families and could afford to have them copied and distributed? Then the book went on to address in detail the source criticism of the Synoptics (this is the part that concerns us). Streeter did not stop there. He went on to deal with the Gospel of John, particularly sensitive. He did all this in a work that was written for undergraduates and that is still in print.

The central section on the Synoptic Problem began with a famous graph that showed his robust British common sense, but mixed with a certain imperial overreach. He begins with Q written in Antioch in AD 50 and with Mark written in Rome in AD 66. This is the simple result of nineteenth-century German scholarship and is the part that should be retained to this day (apart from dates and places that may be correct but are overconfident). Streeter's ambitions were high: to account for everything in the Synoptic Gospels, and to block the idea that if a tradition about Jesus were not found in Q or Mark it was less valuable or sure.[4] So he proposed an M document (material found only in Matthew) and an L source (material found only in Luke, except for the infancy story in Luke 1–2, which came from a separate source). To make things still more complicated, Streeter added a Proto-Luke, which fused Q and L before Mark was included.

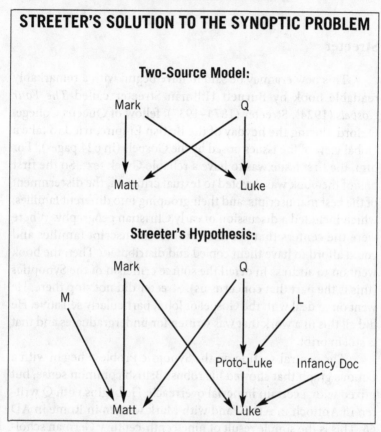

STREETER'S SOLUTION TO THE SYNOPTIC PROBLEM

Two-Source Model:

Mark   Q

Matt   Luke

Streeter's Hypothesis:

M   Mark   Q   L

Proto-Luke   Infancy Doc

Matt   Luke

These hypothetical documents have gone the way of the dodo, except for Q, and for M and L as a kind of shorthand for material peculiar to Matthew or to Luke. The Germans prefer to speak of Matthean or Lucan *Sondergut* (abbreviated SG), meaning "special material." There are still a few who try to maintain the Proto-Luke hypothesis, but they are unlikely to prevail, so far as I can see.

In his chapter on the reconstruction of Q, Streeter recognizes the difficulties of attempts to reconstruct the exact wording of Q. He also frankly admits the absence in Q of the passion narrative. He tries to account for its absence by appealing first to its being handed on by oral tradition in the Q communities and, more dangerously, by affirming that while for Paul the center of the gospel was the cross of Christ, for the other apostles the cross was a scandal, overcome by the resurrection; for them the real hope was the second coming of Christ.[5]

Streeter's graph also provided, in fine print at the bottom, something very valuable. This was a list of verses for each Gospel and for each source. We retain only these: Mark has 661 verses; Matthew, 1068; Luke, 1149; and Q, between 200 and 270. If we take Q and Mark as the two earliest and most reliable sources, and we add them together, we get at least 861 verses of reliable material. Matthew only has 200 or so extra (and less reliable?) verses, among which are the 44 verses in the infancy story. (The infancy stories in Matthew and Luke are commonly regarded as something other than a historical account.) That would mean that much of Matthew is also reliable.

Such a way of proceeding is too simple, because not everything in Q or Mark is flat history, and not everything extra in Matthew or Luke is pure fantasy. There is still a need for critical assessment. For example, the one-verse parable about the treasure hidden in the field (Matt 13:44) is found only in Matthew. Most books on the Gospels and on the parables simply assume it is authentic Jesus material. One could argue against this view on the grounds that the finder sells all that he has for the sake of the kingdom, which is Jesus' teaching on discipleship, found in both Q and Mark and thus doubly attested. Matthew could have invented the parable himself to illustrate Jesus' teaching. But most scholars do not take this route, right or wrong. Streeter's graph gives a rough idea. To that extent it is still useful for students.

Streeter is at his best in his follow-up book *The Primitive Church* (1929). The title is unfortunate. There never was a primitive church in the sense of savage and uneducated. The apostles were born into the Roman Empire, existed under Roman law, benefited from its engineering, and lived with not just biblical but Greek culture all around them (see the Greco-Roman theater at Beth Shean in Galilee, or the Venus at Tel Dan). In this book, Streeter makes it clear that the evangelists were not isolated geniuses locked up in their studies and in mystic trances, but representatives of great churches that paid for the copies and distribution of the Gospels. In this sense, the Gospels are also social products, expressions of local communities, even if addressed ultimately to the whole world, Christian and not yet Christian.

Streeter was teaching at a university that was training administrators for the British Empire at its greatest extent. His work breathes with this sense of the roles of place, communications, and finances, just as in any world movement. To this extent his work was a realistic corrective to the German Romantic cult of the solitary genius (the Evangelist John as a proto-Beethoven). He perhaps was influenced by Justinian's pentarchy of the fifth- to the sixth-century patriarchates (Rome, Antioch, Alexandria, Constantinople, Jerusalem) and by Newman's search for doctrinal witnesses in the different parts of the early Christian world. Streeter risks being an anachronism, because the early Christians often ran scared, due to the persecutions. But that was not their only reality. They wrote books and administered schools and had missions and communications between different centers. So hiding in fear was not their only preoccupation. Streeter sees the more peaceful side of the development.

Burkitt and Manson

We must now leave Oxford and Streeter and take a step backward to prewar Cambridge. Cambridge had a more rigorous approach to the New Testament before Oxford did, due to a trio of scholars: Brooke Westcott, Fenton J. A. Hort, and J. B. Lightfoot.[6]

Bishop Brooke Westcott was the last of the three to die, and as long as he was still alive, the younger members of his school did not dare to publish on the Synoptic Gospels, lest they hurt his extreme love of John. (This would not be the last time that a love of John would hurt Synoptic studies.) But as soon as Westcott was dead (1901), they plunged into the field; Henry Barclay Swete's 1898 commentary on Mark even preceded his death. Then came F. C. Burkitt's *The Gospel History and Its Transmission* (1906).

Burkitt (1864–1935) wrote more for other scholars than for undergraduates, so his appeal was less than Streeter's would later be. However, working in detail and with a historian's curiosity, Burkitt discovered something remarkable: having accepted the two early sources Q and Mark as *independent* of one another, he noticed and studied closely thirty-one cases where this rule is in some sense violated. These are the thirty-one Marcan-Q *overlaps*, cases where Mark and Q seem to be echoing the same teaching of Jesus, but recording it independently one of the other. Mark is not copying Q, Q is not copying Mark. This is the impression one gets when one studies the cases carefully. One concludes that they are two independent witnesses of the same teaching. One could imagine two witnesses to an automobile accident. They have each seen the same event. Each witness reports it in slightly different words, but their testimonies do not differ as to the substance. The litigant who has two such independent witnesses testifying in his favor usually wins the case. The same is true in historical investigation. So Burkitt's contribution is enormous.

After Burkitt presented his list, he concluded, with British understatement and modesty:

> Now I am not going to claim that the list of sayings
> which I have read to you are the deepest or the most
> original of the recorded Sayings of our Lord. It may
> very well be that some of the most profound Sayings of
> His that have survived at all are recorded only by a sin-
> gle Evangelist. But if we are asking what was the teach-

ing of Jesus Christ which impressed His followers generally, or what was the main impression made by His
teaching, then I think we are justified in pointing to
this list that I have drawn up. It may not be the most
profound or subtle view that we can obtain of our
Lord's doctrines, but we have reason to consider it, so
far as it goes, a true view. At least it will be useful to us
as a corrective; any other Portrait of the Lord which we
may draw must not be inconsistent with the Portrait
attested by the mouth of our two witnesses.[7]

This is a moving statement. When one takes a close look at
the thirty-one instances of overlap, a picture of Jesus emerges that
is not unfamiliar. What they have in common is the role of the
Baptist; possibly the baptism of, and certainly the temptation of,
Jesus; his preaching of the kingdom of God and the urgent need to
prepare for it; the gathering of disciples who are then sent on mission and made aware of the risk of persecution; some wisdom
teaching; exorcisms; parables; the search for the messiah and the
Son of man; and conflict with the scribes. Missing are the miracles
(present in both Q and Mark) except for the exorcisms; much of
the teaching; and especially the suffering, death, and resurrection
of Christ, Mark's masterpiece. This picture can count as a critically
assured minimum, but not as the whole story by any means.[8]

Burkitt plays a positive role in this story of the British reception and use of Q. Recently, however, a best-selling book has
appeared by a professional theologian, Janet Martin Soskice of
Cambridge University, that puts Burkitt in a less favorable light.[9] Let
us briefly take note of this. Two wealthy, widowed, gifted, Scottish
twins, Agnes and Margaret Smith (born 1843; Margaret died in
1920, Agnes in 1926), both serious Presbyterians, were interested in
the Bible and in biblical scholarship. They learned all the languages,
ancient and modern, needed to travel to the Sinai to participate in
the discovery and publication of the earliest Syriac versions of the
Gospels, especially the text referred to as *Syriacus Sinaiticus*. Yet

women were still not allowed to take degrees at Cambridge, where the Smiths settled after their voyages of biblical discovery. Burkitt was a young scholar, and he had a hard time acknowledging the right and the ability of the twins to take credit for their discovery and publication of the manuscript. They understandably resented this. Burkitt thus becomes a kind of villain in the Soskice book. There is, however, a sort of reconciliation at the end. Shortly before Agnes's death, Burkitt acknowledged that she was the most learned lady in England. This satisfied her. The list of the Smiths' benefactions is long and ecumenical, although Agnes was not always easy to please. Let us acknowledge this shadow on Burkitt's fair name but not allow it to obscure his many merits.

Once interest in Q had been aroused in the English-speaking world by Streeter and Burkitt, the next thing needed was a commentary. This was provided by T. W. Manson of Manchester University. Manson (1893–1958) decided that a commentary on Q alone would be too short, so he undertook first the commentary on Q, and then continued with commentaries on Streeter's M and L: the teachings of Jesus in Matthew and in Luke that are not in Q or in Mark. This 352-page work, of great utility for a long time, was first published in 1937 in an even larger book that included pieces by two other authors. It was soon realized that the quality of Manson's work and the need it fulfilled required that it be published separately. This work, titled *The Sayings of Jesus* (1949), continues to be reprinted. Manson did not attempt a reconstruction of Q, but printed the Matthew and the Luke versions of each saying or pericope before beginning the commentary. He showed great learning and sound judgment.

The Anti-Q Backlash: Farrer, Goulder, Goodacre, and Watson

Up until this point there had been a steadily expanding general acceptance of Q. But in 1955, an Oxford don decided to try to halt this acceptance. Rev. Austin Farrer (1904–68) of Keble College was primarily a philosophical theologian. But he also tried his hand at a symbolic reading of parts of the New Testament, especially Mark and the Book of Revelation. His eccentric views on the Gospels cost him some promotion, but he continued to be esteemed as a thinker and preacher until his death. In Q studies, he is known for his essay entitled "On Dispensing with Q."[10] Farrer was reacting primarily not to the source criticism of Streeter, but to the form criticism of Rudolf Bultmann and Martin Dibelius. In Farrer's view, they were concentrating on the individual pericopes and losing sight of the evangelists as true authors and theologians. In this sense, Farrer was participating in the next stage of gospel study—redaction criticism—and this is to his honor. As a systematic thinker, he wanted to see the unity of the Gospels, not so much their component parts. And he was willing to sacrifice their historicity in this quest for unity and coherence.

Farrer's main argument against Q was that Luke could have known Matthew directly, without Q. As a logical possibility, this cannot be ruled out. The problem is that editorially it is hard to explain why Luke would have left out so much of Matthew while retaining scattered bits. To answer this objection briefly, Farrer coined the phrase "Luke-pleasingness" to explain why Luke preserved some things and not others. (This category has become even more important in later discussions and emerged as a main issue at the Oxford Conference in 2008.) Here his arguments were flimsy and wallowed in subjectivity.

Michael Goulder (1927–2010) tried to save Farrer's suggestion by making detailed studies of Matthew and Luke, and then writing an article to stop the progress of the general acceptance of Q. He realized that as long as the opponents of "normal science" in this area were represented by W. R. Farmer's rejection of Marcan priority, they would never be taken seriously. So he took Marcan priority as a basis; this got him his foot in the door, so to speak. He also made a concession to the two-source theory, but went only halfway. Then he tried to explain Matthew and Luke without Q.

His Matthew book is quite interesting and worth reading for some of its insights.[11] It is, at its best, an exercise in redaction criticism: How does Matthew rewrite Mark? Goulder's idea is that every time Matthew differs from Mark can be explained as a midrash on Mark. (Midrash in this context means an imaginative or narrative commentary on a received biblical or Jesuanic tradition.) For example, the Lord's Prayer can be explained as midrash on some elements of Jesus' prayer in Gethsemani. This case was, in fact, Goulder's starting point.

There is no doubt that Matthew does indeed at times produce midrashim of Marcan traditions. For example, let us take Mark's remarkable parable of the seed growing secretly (Mark 4:26–27). It used to be said that this was the one parable that neither Matthew nor Luke took up. But now it seems more probable that Matthew rewrote it as the parable of the wheat and the weeds (Matt 13:24–30, 36–43). Another example is when Matthew takes up Mark's verse on forgiveness (Mark 11:25) and includes it in the Sermon on the Mount (Matt 6:14–15), as well as in the parable of the unmerciful servant (Matt 18:21–35). It is easy to see Matthew in this parable as the good pastor or catechist who tries to explain the teaching on forgiveness by composing this parable. So the parable is a midrash by Matthew on Mark. But Goulder goes too far. He wants to explain everything by midrash, nothing by Q.[12] This is the lure of the single solution. His weak arguments are sometimes covered up by bluster and schoolboy cleverness. His rejection of the historicity of everything in Matthew that is not from Mark is a remedy far worse than the illness, if one cares about historicity at all. Goulder's gift for mathematics and his feel for literary form allow him no sense of the difference between bare, abstract possibility and high historical probability. One senses that for Goulder the Gospel of Matthew is not a book for the nourishing of the life of a community of believers, but a curiosity, a dead cat useful for anatomical dissection and the exploration of logical possibilities.

Goulder's lengthy book on Luke undertakes the same purpose. It is a study of Luke's use of Mark and Matthew, and thus Luke becomes a midrash on Matthew. This project involves Goulder in some very complex, ingenious guesses as to how Luke worked. There are two main objections to this view. First, it is too complex in comparison with the idea that Luke is simply quoting an earlier source called Q. (The Q that Luke quotes is free of Matthean redactional preferences such as the *kingdom of heaven* instead of the *kingdom of God*. This is why scholars generally prefer the Lucan wording to the Matthean wording as representing the earlier, simpler version of the saying of Jesus in Q.) The second objection to Goulder's view is that it presupposes Luke working in a way foreign to ancient scribal practices of compostion.[13] This way of working, "unpicking" what is in Matthew to make something quite different, is sometimes called an effort to unscramble the egg.

Goulder's last major attempt to stop the triumph of the Q corollary[14] was the article "Is Q a Juggernaut?" The title is its theme: Is Q being used as a bulldozer to flatten and thus destroy all alternative hypotheses? Goulder feared that it was. His essay is like a final throw of the dice to save his alternative, and it contains very varied arguments. Discussing all of them would take us too far afield, so we must be selective. However, we will note that his list of reasons why people hold on to the Q corollary does not even mention the main one: interest in history. Theologically he has a hard time imagining that some Christians could find Matthew's theology generally appealing, even though at times troubling in detail, such as the fate of the villains in parables.

Goulder's trump card that proves Luke knew Matthew is the verse that has become a famous battleground, so we should mention it. In Jesus' interrogation by the Sanhedrin in the passion narrative, Mark describes the soldiers blindfolding Jesus and beating him (Mark 14:65). Matthew and Luke both add to this description using the same, *identically worded* sentence: "*Tis estin ho paisas se?*" "Who is it that struck you?" (Matt 26:68; Luke 22:64). Even though the sentence is short, it can hardly be an accident or coincidence. Can this case alone suffice to bring down the two-source hypothesis? When it comes down to a single exception, historians hesitate to draw sweeping conclusions. They prefer multiple attestation. It is too easy to provide alternative explanations for a single case, for example, oral tradition.[15]

Goulder also invokes K. R. Popper's idea of a scientifically *useful* hypothesis as one that can be falsified. If it cannot be falsified, we can never know for absolute certain if it is true or not. This way of reasoning is true in mathematics. If there were a case where $2 + 2 = 5$, the proposition of normal mathematics that $2 + 2 = 4$ would be falsified. But one black swan would not falsify the normal truth that swans are generally white. In Japan, they say that a geisha as such is not a prostitute, yet a virginal geisha is as rare as a white crow. There is also an ambiguity in the word *useful*. A bit of evidence could be *useless* for logic, but still *useful* for history. For example, a medically useful hypothesis like the circulation of the blood could conceivably have an exceptional case where the blood does not circulate. But this would not prevent doctors from using this theory to save lives. We cannot be absolutely, mathematically certain that Luke used Matthew rather than Q, but on the balance of probabilities, it seems more probable that he used Q rather than Matthew directly. Streeter warned that Q cannot be reconstructed in minute detail. In a free society, scholars are free to try to reconstruct it, but the user—the reader, the student—should not be deceived that it is entirely accurate. It is only a humanly fallible attempt.

The cause of Farrer-Goulder was far from defeated, however. Goulder could die content, because his crusade had been taken up by a competent student of his. In 2002, Mark S. Goodacre (b. 1967) published his dissertation, *The Case Against Q: Studies in Markan Priority and the Synoptic Problem*.[16] Goodacre frames his argument in this way: Once you grant the postulate that Luke knew the text of Matthew's Gospel, you have no need to postulate a sayings source. Or, as I prefer to say, if you can show that it is *more probable* that Luke used Matthew in such a way as to result in his own Gospel (while leaving out many things in Matthew), than that he used a sayings source, then you have won your case. *More probable* here means "more natural," "more simple," and "more self-evident."

In the past, one would argue that Luke changed something from his sources because he had a different theology. But much in Goodacre's argument depends upon certain assumptions about Luke's aesthetic preferences. This dependence upon aesthetics corresponds with a modern trend toward aesthetics in biblical studies. This dependence is also due to the literary turn in biblical studies and to the influence of Hans Urs von Balthasar in theology. There is no doubt that Luke has a sense of beauty beyond that of the other Synoptic evangelists. But he is not all sweetness and light, as Dante had suggested by calling him the evangelist of the *mansuetudo Christi*, the meekness of Christ. Luke (and Q) have a robust, tough side that does not suit modern soft preferences. For example, Luke has the woes after the Beatitudes; this is less happy-clappy than Matthew, whether Luke composed the woes himself or copied them from a source. Luke includes the demand to leave one's wife, along with the other demands for being a disciple; Matthew and Mark do not do this. Luke is also quite tough on the demands for poverty and simplicity. Even the Magnificat has harsh words for the arrogant. All this means that Luke might not have been so quick to get rid of the painful features in Matthew, had he known of them, as some modern critics suppose.[17]

Goodacre's case, stripped of the clearing-up of popular mis-understandings, comes down to whether Luke's using and not using Matthew to write his Gospel makes more sense than his using Q. One detail in this case is that Luke did not use Matthew 16:17–19 ("Thou art Peter"), explained as Luke not liking Peter or wanting to take him down a peg. But in fact Luke gives plenty of space to Peter in the Gospel, and even more in the first twelve chapters of Acts. John S. Kloppenborg's response to Goodacre gives a good statement of the facts.[18] I myself began with the prejudice that Luke did not like Peter. But my prejudice has been overcome by a slow reading of Acts 10–11, wherein Peter's arrival in Caesarea to deal with the Cornelius case is portrayed as almost an imperial *parousia* and where Peter is treated with more than ordinary human respect.

In general, we may say that Matthew is the teacher-friendly handbook. The Christian teacher can find what he or she is looking for there, because Matthew has collected the teaching of Jesus into five or more great discourses. Luke, on the other hand, is the great narrator. His unique contribution is the travel narrative, which runs from Luke 9:51 to 19:27. It is long, loosely structured picaresque. Bible students have a harder time finding things they like or want to find in this section of the Gospel. For example, certain of Luke's favorite themes—like prayer, discipleship, repentance, or even Samaritans—are scattered throughout the section. But that is not the whole truth. There *are* a few groupings or thematic collections within this flood of material of all sorts: A teaching on meals, hospitality, and invitations is gathered in Luke 14:1–24. The three parables of mercy are found in Luke 15:3–32. Also, there is much talk of money and riches in chapter 16.

It is not hard to imagine Luke using Mark as a framework and then integrating Q material into that framework as he goes along. Furthermore, he adds material from his own oral or written sources, often as prolongations or commentaries on what he has received from these two main sources. But for Luke to have broken up Matthew's well-constructed accounts to scatter the material the way Goodacre proposes is less easy to imagine. F. Gerald Downing, in two articles, argues that ancient historians do not conflate different sources in the way that Goulder and Goodacre suppose Luke must have done if he only had Matthew and Mark before him. Ancient authors like Josephus and Plutarch conflate only in a simple way, not unpicking bits and pieces as Luke supposedly did, but simply using one version to supplement another; and where they disagree, choosing one of the two or making up one's own third version.[19] Goodacre's Luke rolls to and from his copy of Matthew by splicing, creating a detailed collage. Downing claims that this way of proceeding is anachronistic, without ancient analogy. But Francis B. Watson (b. 1956) of Durham University tries once again to examine the matter.

Watson's study of Q's methodology[20] begins and concludes neutrally. He only claims to consider issues of method. He does not adjudicate. On the other hand, he says that his argument tends in the direction of returning Q to the limbo of possibilities and probabilities and even total rejection. He is sympathetic to Goodacre. Although he does not invoke it, behind his argument stands the principle of Occam's razor, that beings are not to be multiplied beyond necessity. Q is a hypothetical being. Watson coins the abbreviation L/M for the Goodacre view that Luke used Matthew. If the L/M hypothesis is more plausible than Q, then it should prevail because it is simpler; it requires no extra entity. (However, Watson cheats a bit. He at first says that if Q can produce a more intelligible, coherent, and plausible account than its rival, then it is reasonable to accord it a fact-like status. But just pages later he lowers the standards for L/M: it only needs to be "no less plausible" than the alternative. Presumably the lower standard or bar is justified by Occam's razor of greater simplicity, but Watson does not say this.)

Watson then tackles Q in three sections, as it is found in Matthew chapters 3 to 4, then 5 to 7, then 8 to 12. The first of these sections deals with the preaching of John the Baptist and the temptation of Jesus (paralleled in Luke 3 to 4). Watson says that the beginning of Q is hard to fix, since both Matthew and Luke insert Q material into a Marcan framework as a supplement.[21] The terrain is slippery. Since the beginning of Q is lost, it is hard to be certain about Mark's procedure. One view is that Mark knew Q. Nevertheless, the longer temptation narrative in Matthew and Luke support the Q hypothesis, if one thinks that the temptation story has an early character, as suggested by the work of Birger Gerhardsson.[22] The second section (Matthew 5 to 7; parallel Luke 6 and bits of 11 to 16) deals with the Great Discourse. If here Luke is using Matthew, he drastically reduces the Sermon on the Mount to roughly a third of what he found in his source. (On this theory, Q is

Matthew on a diet.) Luke then extracts thirteen items from the Sermon on the Mount and puts them in chapters 11, 12, 13, 14, and 16; that is, all in his travel narrative. Watson also notes the phenomenon of alternating primitivity: Luke seems to offer a more primitive or earlier form of Jesus' teaching on poverty, but poverty is also one of Luke's redactional interests, so his version could be either primary or tertiary—in the Beatitudes, for example. This is carefully stated, but Luke's emphasis on poverty had to start from somewhere, so it seems more reasonable to think that he derived it from Q, as offering a close rendering of Jesus' own teaching. Watson recognizes that more primitive could mean more authentic, that is, Jesus' very own words. He then quotes Jens Schroeter: "What we can get is the remembered Jesus, as the content of the social memories of early Christianity."[23] This may be a true, sophisticated, modish way of putting it, but it may not quite satisfy someone who asks: Did Jesus really say this? Or, What did Jesus say? In any case, here again the Q hypothesis gives a more satisfactory, easily intelligible account of what Matthew and Luke have done than the alternative.

Watson finally considers the common sequence in Matthew 8–12 // Luke 7–11, especially Matthew chapters 8 to 9. Luke has here better preserved the Q sequence, because Matthew has deliberately chosen to gather ten miracle stories together after the Great Sermon, to show that Jesus is Messiah both in word and deed. Watson notes this common view but rejects it as an explanation of Luke's arrangement. Watson recognizes that Matthew's handling of Mark and Q is at times puzzling, as would be Luke's use of Matthew if he did indeed use him. Much is not obvious on either hypothesis. (We should be grateful when we get some clarity, as in the case of Matthew 8 to 10 and the ten miracles.)

Watson may be right that Luke reveres Mark more than he reveres Q or Matthew. But he does not say that Matthew may revere Q more than he reveres Mark, even though both Matthew and Luke have incorporated Q into a Marcan narrative framework. Yet this may well be the case, as Matthew's care with his five discourses suggests. Watson admits that one can always speculate on why *x* did *y* to *z*. Sometimes our speculations are more easy to see as correct; at other times they are less certainly convincing. What seems clear is that on Watson's own showing, L/M is not vastly more perspicacious than the account given on the Q hypothesis. The contrary is the case. Perhaps that is why his conclusion is muted and modest.

Pro-Q Support Continues: Tuckett, Catchpole, and the Oxford Symposium

In the British Isles, there are a number of professors who are pro-Q, notably Christopher Tuckett of Oxford and David Catchpole of Exeter. Tuckett's main book about Q first introduces the state of Q research.[24] The main thesis of the book is that Q is the document of an early Jewish-Christian group angered at the apathetic response of others to its preaching. Q draws together prophetic and sapiential traditions to speak meaningfully of their rejection, and eschatological materials to speak of the impending judgment that awaits all who do not embrace the coming kingdom. Tuckett focuses on Q as we have it, without committing himself to multiple layers in the growth of Q. He also refuses to claim for Q verses where there is not double attestation. Q's Christology for him includes Jesus as Wisdom's rejected prophet and as the persecuted, suffering Son of man. Q's Jesus is best understood as an eschatological prophet, in the tradition of Isaiah. Tuckett is so cautious and well grounded that there is little to criticize. The idea of anger at an apathetic response is interesting but speculative and not necessary to explain the judgment material. That Jesus in many ways was influenced by and stood in the line of Isaiah need hardly be doubted. But this truth should not be used to avoid the Danielic, apocalyptic dimension, which itself combines wisdom and prophecy and is closer to Jesus' theme of the kingdom of God.

Another careful, prudent Q scholar is David Catchpole. His

main work on Q consists of a series of special studies that are characterized by sober analysis.[25] There is never any doubt for Catchpole that Q exists, so it is not the Goulder tack. For example, his study of the healing of the centurion's servant never doubts that even in Q it was a miracle.[26] Catchpole does go out on a limb, however, when dealing with the difficult question of how Q began.[27] He makes a very clear case for Mark having known Q and having carefully rewritten its version of the beginning of the Gospel with a quote from Isaiah 40 and John the Baptist. The real problems with the beginning of Q make it understandable why some prefer to begin it with the Beatitudes. Catchpole also throws the normal way of thinking of Mark and Q as independent early sources into disarray, which would weaken the historical value of the doubly attested sayings. Perhaps the best argument against Mark knowing and using Q is that a close look at the doubly attested sayings convinces the reader that Mark is not copying from Q at all but reproducing oral tradition.

We may conclude this chapter on the British contribution to the study of Q with a reference to the stately volume *New Studies in the Synoptic Problem*. They are studies gathered to honor C. M. Tuckett on his sixtieth birthday, first given at an Oxford Conference in April 2008. Most of the studies are not about Q. The contributors were chosen to be representative of various points of view, and were further told not to pull their punches, yet one has the impression that the organization is for the most part in the hands of those who maintain the two-source solution. One of the points made is that the study of the Synoptic Gospels has to be broadened to include the contributions of John, the various longer endings of Mark (including for some the expansion found in Clement of Alexandria), the *Gospel of Thomas* and other non-canonical gospels, and the Apostolic Fathers. This is perfectly true and not all brand new. In his fair and careful introductory chapter on the current state of the Synoptic Problem, Tuckett reminds us that all our solutions are provisional. He concludes: "Even though I have (unashamedly?!) sought in this paper to argue that the weaknesses of the 2DH[28] are possibly less than those of other competing hypotheses today, I hope that I have shown that this theory too is open to questioning."[29] He denies absolute certainty on this as on other points. (He means, I suspect, mathematical certainty, a kind of certainty inappropriate to this type of literary-historical inquiry. In history a highly probable, useful hypothesis can attain to a fact-like status.) Tuckett's caution could be taken as merely stylistic courtesy, but it could also signify the eroding of a consensus, if the extremely late dating of Luke-Acts by scholars like Richard Pervo would prevail. If Luke were writing around AD 120, it is hard to imagine he would not know of Matthew, written, it is commonly said, around AD 90.[30]

Goodacre raises another objection we should consider. He says that the Q hypothesis reeks of nineteenth-century historiography with its search for reliable sources. It is out of date, old-fashioned. The Synoptic Problem requires a new look, even if the new look faces insuperable hurdles of literary and historical improbability. On this point we may cite from scholar Gilbert Highet's ambitious work *The Classical Tradition*:

> The false parallel with science caused many… errors… in classical study. One odd one was the habit of *Quellenforschung*, the search for sources, which began as a legitimate inquiry into the material used by a poet, historian, or philosopher, and was pushed to the absurd point at which it was assumed that everything in a poem, even such a poem such as the *Aeneid*, was derived from earlier writers. It is a typical scientific assumption that everything can be explained by synthesis, but it omits the essential artistic fact of creation.[31]

One could parry this charge in several ways. Highet denounces exaggeration. The classic two-source theory exercises sober restraint. It postulates, in addition to Mark, only one substantial source, present in both Matthew and Luke. It is supported in this by Luke's statement that he consulted several sources. Highet has an aesthetic bias and is interested in artistic creation. Well and good, but this does not exclude an interest in historical fact and truth, all the more so in the study of a text that determines the conduct of so many lives. The Q postulate leaves plenty of room for the evangelists' creativity, especially in the case of parables created by them in order to explain Jesus' teachings. Nor does it exclude supplementary material from oral tradition. It just notices some material that seems to bear a family resemblance and provides a historical basis from which the subsequent creativity can take its start, a basis that enables us to distinguish fact from fiction, at least to some extent.

Text Study: A Marcan-Q Overlap on Discipleship

The point of this chapter's example is for the reader to see the reality of Mark and Q as two early and independent sources of the teaching and practice of Jesus, as well as to sense the variants that occur when sayings are transmitted orally, variants that affect the wording but not the sense or gist. The example is thus an education in historical detection.

We begin with a set of sayings which occur twice in Matthew and Luke, once as copied from Mark and once as copied from Q. The Q version or Luke 14:26–27 (// Matt 10:37–38) reads:

> "If anyone comes to me and does not hate father and mother [and wife] and daughter, that one cannot be my disciple. And whoever does not take his cross and come after me, cannot be my disciple."

The Marcan version reads:

> Jesus said, "Amen I say to you, there is no one who has left house or brothers or sisters or mother or father or

children or lands, for my sake and for the gospel, who will not receive a hundredfold now in this time, houses and brothers and sisters and mothers and children and lands, with persecution, and in the age to come eternal life."

That is Mark 10:29–30. Earlier in Mark (8:34b) we find:

"If anyone would come after me, let him deny himself and take up his cross and follow me."

These Marcan sayings are reproduced in Matthew 19:29 (somewhat lightened):

"And everyone who has left houses or brothers or sisters or father or mother or children or lands, for my name's sake, will receive a hundredfold, and inherit eternal life."

and in Luke 18:29–30:

And he said to them, "Truly, I say to you, there is no man who has left house or wife or brothers or parents or children, for the sake of the kingdom of God, who will not receive manifold more in this time, and in the age to come eternal life."

Why did Matthew and Luke reproduce these sayings twice, in two slightly different versions? The short answer is that Matthew and Luke each thought that these sayings were important for, characteristic of, and determinative for the Jesus movement, and they each also decided independently to reproduce the sayings more or less as they found them in their two main sources, Q and Mark. Historians and believers may be grateful for their care. Historically it is as certain that Jesus said something like this as anything else related in the Gospel stories or as anything else in world history.

The Q form of the saying has the verb *hate* in the sense of *to love less* (Rom 9:13, from Mal 1:3–4). The Q form is undoubtedly original, and is frequently altered out of sensitivity to readers' refinement. The Lucan form of Q includes the wife among the family members to be renounced; whether that too is original is also debated. Q is missing the verb for *to deny oneself* from the second saying; this omission can be explained by the placement just after the first verse, which renders the verb *deny* unnecessary. Although there are some parallels to this renunciation of family in earlier Jewish tradition, the verses remain shocking. Jesus evidently felt that there was great eschatological urgency and that in the circumstances he had the authority to make such a demand.

The verse in Q about taking up one's cross speaks of the necessity of suffering as an element in the life of the disciples. The verse employs the metaphor of the cross. The authenticity of the verse has been challenged on the grounds that, prior to Jesus' crucifixion, such a figure of speech would have been unintelligible; the saying is therefore post-Easter. This challenge is easy to overcome. Crucifixion was a widespread punishment in both the Persian Empire and the Roman Empire, a part of common experience. Part of the Jewish catechetical instruction on the Shema confession of faith included willingness to undergo martyrdom for the love of God, if necessary. Cross-bearing as a metaphor is used by the pagan Stoic philosopher Epictetus: "If you want to be crucified, just wait. The cross will come. If it seems reasonable to comply…, then it is to be carried through, and your integrity maintained" (Epictetus, *Diss.*, 2.2.20). It is safe to conclude that this saying is independent of the passion story (not recounted in Q) and uses a profane Greek metaphor.

When we look at Mark 10:29–30, we see a quite different echo of the same basic demand for the disciple to renounce family ties. Mark regards the saying as so important that he loads it up with all kinds of supplementary remarks. The sentence moves from being a condition to being a declaration. It is solemnly introduced with the Amen formula. The listing of renunciations now begins with the comprehensive word *oikia*, "family," which includes buildings and business, as well as people, as the governing concept. Siblings and land are then added, as is the explicit double motivation: "for my sake and for the gospel." Then comes the major new element of a long reward clause: a hundredfold in this age, but also persecutions, then eternal life in the world to come.

The persecution obviously looks to the post-Easter situation of martyrdom. The earthly hundredfold looks to the Christian community. In the reward clause, one receives back all one's kin except the father. This may be so because the disciple is now the head of a new community. Viewed as a whole, the verses are an important statement that attests to the unconditionality and God-centeredness of Jesus' call to follow.

When we compare Q and Mark, we see they have in common that the disciple or follower must leave his family, take up his cross, and come after Jesus. In other words, they each echo Jesus' call for radical discipleship, in terms calculated to arrest attention and to offend sensibilities. This is why they were remembered.

As for historicity, doubts have been expressed about the developed form in Mark, but not for the kernel that it shares with Q. One could say that Mark tames the radicalism of Q, not in the sense that he knew Q as a written document but in the sense that he inherited a radical oral tradition. Mark is not copying Q; he is echoing a common tradition. Once we see the high probability of the authenticity of the kernel of these sayings, we gain a valuable insight into Jesus' own self-understanding and method of operating. By calling men and women to such a radical loyalty, he gave his movement its shape and enabled it to survive the first hostile reactions it met.

A SAYING ON DISCIPLESHIP AND A MARCAN-Q OVERLAP

A saying on discipleship from the oral tradition and inherited by the written traditions of Q and Mark:

The sayings from Q and Mark are repeated twice in Matthew and Luke:

Q 14:26–27

If anyone comes to me and does not *hate father and mother and daughter*, that one cannot be my disciple. And whoever does not take his cross and come after me, cannot be my disciple.

Mark 8:34b

"If anyone would come after me, let him deny himself and take up his cross and **follow me.**"

Mark 10:29–30

Jesus said, "Amen, I say to you, there is no one *who has left house (oikia) or brother or sisters or mother or father or children* or lands, for my sake and for the gospel, [30] who will not *receive a hundredfold,* now in this time, houses and brothers and sisters and mothers and children and lands, with persecution, and in the age to come *eternal life.*"

Matthew 10:37–38 (NRSV)

[37] "Whoever *loves father or mother more than me* is not worthy of me; and whoever loves son or *daughter more than me* is not worthy of me; [38] and whoever does not take up the cross and **follow me** is not worthy of me."

Matthew 19:29 (NRSV)

[29] "And everyone who has left houses (*oikias*) or brothers or sisters or father or mother or children or fields, for my name's sake, will *receive a hundredfold,* and will inherit *eternal life.*"

Luke 14:26–27

[26] "Whoever comes to me and does not *hate father and mother,* wife and *children,* brothers and sisters, yes, and even life itself, cannot be my disciple. [27] Whoever does not carry the cross and **follow me** cannot be my disciple."

Luke 18:29–30 (NRSV)

[29] And he said to them, "Truly I tell you, there is no one *who has left house (oikia) or wife or brothers or parents or children,* for the sake of the kingdom of God, [30] who will *not get back very much more* in this age, and in the age to come *eternal life.*"

4

THE CATHOLIC RECEPTION OF THE Q POSTULATE

The Political Background

Although this chapter title seems to switch our report on Q studies from geography to confessional theology, this is only partly true. In effect it will begin with a French report and a Roman (Italo-German) reaction, and then broaden out to Belgium and Roman Catholic Germany. It is usual in histories of the reception of the historical-critical method in biblical studies in the Roman Catholic Church to give a place of honor to the French Dominican priest Marie-Joseph Lagrange (1855–1938), founder of the École Biblique, the French biblical and archaeological school in Jerusalem. His is one of the heroic stories in modern Catholic history:[1] his undeserved sufferings were considerable, and many pray for his speedy beatification. It is natural to begin with him; however, this should not lead us to ignore the contributions of some of his contemporaries, notably Alfred Loisy (1857–1940).

The reception of the Q postulate among French Catholics may seem to have nothing to do with politics. Unfortunately that is not so. We will try to sketch the situation in broad strokes. French Catholics were divided among themselves for over a century as to how to view their Revolution of 1789. Many rallied around the nobility loyal to the House of Bourbon, which wanted a total rejection of the Revolution. Other Catholics rallied around the House of Orleans, which partially accepted the Revolution and the modernity that went with it: in politics, a constitutional monarchy with a sovereign parliament and a tolerance of different philosophies and religions; and in culture, a limited acceptance of, among other things, the historical-critical method in studying the past.

As if that were not enough to worry about, French Catholics were also concerned about checking the rise of an aggressive, militaristic Prussia, which happened to have a very good high school system and flourishing universities in which there were state faculties of theology, both Protestant and Catholic—and this at a time when all French universities had seen their theological faculties closed. After the humiliating defeat at the hands of a united Germany in 1871, the French thought of revenge. French seminarians interested in the Bible and the early church came to see the weaknesses of their own formation in comparison with what was available across the Rhine. Some of them decided to devote their lives to redeeming French honor in these fields of study. But to do so, they first had to learn the newer methods and discoveries of their rivals. Two attitudes evolved. The attitude that generally represented Lagrange's opponents said: *If learning comes from the enemy, it must be bad and we must reject it.* The other attitude said, in effect: *We must accept what is sound in our rivals' learning and then go on to do our own work.* Lagrange was from a politically liberal, Orleanist family, and before becoming a priest he was first trained as a lawyer. He represented the second of these two attitudes, which was undoubtedly part of his motivation to found an institute for biblical study.

The French Catholic Reception of Q: Lagrange, Loisy, and De Solages

In 1890, Marie-Joseph Lagrange founded the École Biblique et Archéologique Française de Jérusalem. It had a simple program based on a pun: we must read the document (the Bible) in the light of the monument (the archaeological discoveries that were beginning to pour in). The school was founded at a time when the Ottoman Empire was in a weakened state. There was a rush by the Western powers to acquire property in the Near East, especially in Jerusalem. Britain, France, the United States, Russia, and Germany were all involved—even Italy, Spain, and Greece in their own ways. A French republican government, which persecuted the church at home, supported the church abroad because it served to extend their prestige and their culture. Lagrange's school was the first *permanent* school of modern biblical and archaeological research and the only one that attempted to have a complete library in the Holy Land, and to give classes and degrees. All of the foreign schools undertook archaeological investigations. The inscriptions were waiting in the farmers' fields for them to be copied and published.

At first both Lagrange and Alfred Loisy were interested in the problems regarding the Old Testament, especially Genesis and Exodus, arising from discoveries of Babylonian texts that told of a great flood that sounded like the Noah story and of law codes that sounded like the laws given to Moses. One of Lagrange's collaborators, Vincent Scheil, published the first printed edition of Hammurabi's Code with a translation. The stone code stands proudly today in the Louvre in Paris. Lagrange rode out into the Sinai desert during his first year in the Holy Land to measure and trace the route of the exodus. He got the impression that a literal reading would not solve all the problems. He thus early gave up the idea that archaeology would "prove" the Bible in the least detail. A more modern approach was required.

Such views were not to the liking of political and religious conservatives. The Bourbon restorationists wanted no compromise with the world that arose after the Revolution. Some theologians, using a mathematical, or Cartesian, model of reason, thought that if the Bible were seen to be in error on even the most trivial point of geography, its whole saving message would crumble into ruin. Lagrange's work was at first favorably received and was encouraged by the aging Pope Leo XIII, who established the Pontifical Biblical Commission for biblical studies in 1902. But a sharp change came under Pius X with his 1907 decree against modernism, *Lamentabili Sane*, a sort of "syllabus of errors." Biblical scholarship was severely restricted, at first in the area of the Old Testament. Lagrange decided to give up work on the Hebrew Bible (his commentary on Genesis remains in manuscript). He turned to the Gospels, where he felt he could in good conscience be quite conservative. But he aroused the wrath of a German Jesuit, Leopold Fonck, who campaigned against him from a base in Rome. Fonck never represented all Jesuits or all German Catholic biblical scholars. But for a time he caused a great deal of trouble for Lagrange.

In his commentary on Mark of 1911, Lagrange began by accepting the modern critical view that it is the first of the four canonical Gospels to be written. In other words, he was accepting Holtzmann's first principle, Marcan priority. The second step was inevitable: what is one to make of the double tradition, the material that Matthew and Luke have in common that is not in Mark? Lagrange was more reserved in regard to the Q postulate. He had difficulty imagining such a collection of sayings of Jesus reproduced without context. (The *Gospel of Thomas* had not yet been discovered in its entirety.) He then proceeded to understand Papias's statement as speaking of an "Aramaic Matthew" that was substantially identical with our "Greek Matthew" but included especially the sayings and teachings of Jesus.[2] This became the Catholic version of the two-source hypothesis. This version "slipped through" the tenth decree of the Pontifical Biblical Commission, which we will treat next. Lagrange would go on to call this version the *logia* or sometimes even Q. Others called it Proto-Matthew. In practice, it often differed from the normal two-source theory in name only, especially when the enforcement of the decree was relaxed. It continued to be mentioned until 1955, when the decrees of the commission were no longer obligatory to hold. Then this "Catholic version" was quietly dropped.[3]

The success of Lagrange's moderate version is astounding when we consider the relevant decree itself. The first nine decrees of the Pontifical Biblical Commission deal with the Old Testament, except the fourth, which deals with the Gospel According to John, and the ninth, with the evaluation of students of Sacred Scripture. The next set of decrees, ten to sixteen, issued between 1911 and 1915, deal with the New Testament. (The decree style peters out with one more in 1933, as by then it was realized that biblical problems could not be solved or adequately dealt with by the decree format.)

The tenth decree is the one that concerns us. It is about Matthew. Section 4 of the decree asks whether it is probable that Matthew composed a collection of sayings and discourses of Christ (this is an allusion to Q), and the answer is in the negative. In section 5, the substantial identity of the Greek and the vernacular (Hebrew or Aramaic) versions of Matthew is affirmed. In section 7, the historical authenticity of certain texts of great importance to dogma, notably concerning the primacy of Peter (Matt 16:17–19) and the Great Commission (28:19–20), is affirmed. The decree is dated June 19, 1911, shortly after Lagrange's commentary on Mark came out. The decree prevented Catholic scholars who wanted to be considered orthodox from openly embracing Q until 1955.[4]

This decree was not aimed primarily at Lagrange, but at Loisy, who in 1907 had published a complete commentary on the Synoptic Gospels in two fat volumes.[5] Loisy simply read the Greek Gospel Synopsis, guided by the two-source hypothesis, and quickly wrote a straightforward but well-informed commentary on the whole text. His work was rapidly accepted as a solid guide by serious scholars of the main confessions. It represented the reading of the texts such as was made possible by the learning of the time. It was neither boldly progressive nor very conservative, but it was up-to-date, and it had the advantage of being in French, accessible to many who did not know German. He was still working within the Catholic doctrinal tradition, but without taking manual dogmatic theology as the principal norm. If we take a cheerful, providentialist view of what happened once he was excommunicated (1908), we can say that Loisy expressed the scholarly truth in a plain straightforward way in French, but now outside institutional church circles. Lagrange on the other hand said only as much of the truth as he could get by the censors of the day, in a tortured cautious way, his works always bearing an imprimatur. He stayed and suffered within the institution of his day. Each scholar served the sacred cause of biblical truth in his own way. Both had to wait for better times after their deaths, at least several decades, when such divisions of labor were no longer necessary. As the Queen of Hearts says in *Alice in Wonderland*, "All have won and all shall have prizes."[6] (After his excommunication, Loisy became bitter and said heretical things; however, this was not so at the time of his commentary on the Synoptics.)

Lagrange had many remarkable disciples. One was the southern French nobleman and priest Bruno de Solages (1895–1983), gifted in mathematics, interested in science. He became rector of the private French Catholic university in Toulouse for nearly forty years. He denounced the deportation of the Jews during the Second World War and therefore was himself deported by the Nazis. He also resisted the persecution of the priest-scientist Teilhard de Chardin. As a student of Lagrange in Jerusalem, de Solages had learned about the two-source theory. That means Q— and he accepted the theory. Once the Pontifical Biblical Commission decrees were no longer in effect, de Solages did all he could to publicize in French the usefulness of Q, writing a series of books both technical and popular. In the most popular of them, an accessible short paperback, he provides what is probably the first French translation/presentation of Q.[7] His presentation was so persuasive that even very conservative theologians were won over. (I base this sentence on personal experience in Europe.) Other disciples of Lagrange also remained faithful to him as a master teacher and were able to win posthumous victories for him in other areas: Bonsirven on the kingdom of God; Tisserant, Guitton, and Voste on the genres of Genesis 1–11; de Vaux and Benoit on biblical inerrancy.

The German Catholic Reception of Q: Schmid, Wikenhauser, and Hoffmann

In Catholic Germany, Josef Schmid (1893–1975) did a serious study of the Synoptic Problem in 1930.[8] By a careful observation of the sequence of pericopes in each Gospel, he was convinced that the two-source hypothesis was correct and that all the other alternatives could be refuted. This technical work laid the groundwork for the German Catholic acceptance of the two-source solution.[9] The acceptance was diffused through the widely used textbook by his senior colleague Alfred Wikenhauser (1883–1960).[10] Once this handbook was translated into English, the simplicity of the solution gained it wide acceptance among American Catholics.

Meanwhile the next generation of German Catholic Q scholars proceeded to do more detailed work. Notable among these is Paul Hoffmann of Bamberg. He pushed the literary analysis of Q sayings to a point where some hesitated to follow him.[11] He also drew fairly radical and polemically stated theological conclusions not always endorsed by his students. As a concerned priest in the church, he recently published a collection of his essays on Jesus and the early church.[12] For Hoffmann, Jesus was the prophetic messenger of the kingdom of God. Jesus transgressed boundaries to create an integrating and inclusive community, and his community possessed an egalitarian ethos as a circle of disciples. Jesus had a simple faith in God as Abba, who affirms human life. Jesus called his disciples to a practice proposed in the Sermon on the Mount. This practice culminates in an ethics of peace, an active love of enemies.

Despite some hesitation concerning Hoffman, Q studies were taken seriously by a growing number of German Catholic scholars.

Sancta Mater Ecclesia: Precursor to
Vatican II's *Dei Verbum*

We should pause here to note a development that occurred at the time of the Second Vatican Council. As the different documents of the Council were being prepared, it was generally recognized that one of the most important would be on the sources of revelation—in brief, Scripture and Tradition. Even though the document did not need to be long, it was fiercely debated in detail, and was only approved in its final form in the last session of the Council in 1965. As the debates were going on, the experts realized that a preliminary document needed to be worked out that would prepare the way for the acceptance of this dogmatic constitution both inside and outside of the Council. As a result, in 1964 the Pontifical Biblical Commission issued a crucial document on the nature of the historical truth of the Gospels, called *Sancta Mater Ecclesia.*[13] (Its chief authors are reportedly Lucien Cerfaux, Beda Rigaux, Rudolf Schnackenburg, and Xavier Leon-Dufour.) Its release was at first hush-hush, and even after its use in the Council, it did not get the attention it deserves. It tries in a few pages to summarize the assured results of New Testament studies that had taken place since the twenties and thirties of the twentieth century and to integrate them into official church teaching. This concerns primarily form criticism and redaction criticism, which are not our concern. But form and redaction criticism presuppose the two-source solution of the Synoptic Problem, so the issue of Q is implicit in the discussion. This document did the work for which it was intended, even though it did not solve every problem raised, for example, the issue of myth in the Bible. However, it was a step forward. What is important for us here is that the document of the Biblical Commission did not take a formal stand on the Synoptic Problem. The members wanted to leave this question open. They hoped they could express themselves sufficiently generically so that what they said about historicity would be applicable no matter which source solution was adopted. This led them to some hasty oversimplifications.

What should we make of this? On the one hand, it is probably a good thing that the Pontifical Biblical Commission should not have tried to settle such technical matters in detail. Let the scholars have their legitimate freedom to explore and to debate. On the other hand, not taking a stand often results in blurred pictures of Jesus and the work of the evangelists. Such blurring can lead to lazy, facile conclusions that are not well founded and can deceive the unwitting faithful, so there is a risk involved. Strictly speaking, no professional biblical scholarship or theology is necessary to be saved. Faith, hope, and charity suffice. But there is a place for educated Christians to explain their faith in dialogue with modern problematics. The transmission of the faith can be hindered if this activity of education is not fostered.

The Flemish Belgian Reception of Q: Neirynck

The University of Leuven has been a center of Catholic theology since 1425. It lies in Belgian Flanders, where Dutch is spoken, although English is often used for its scholarly publications. (In French, the town is known as Louvain. When the university split into two campuses based on language in 1966, the Dutch-speaking Flemings got the old university town, while the French-speaking Walloons built a new campus some miles away.)

The key figure for our subject is Frans Neirynck (1927–2012). A professor at Leuven for over thirty years (1960–92), he has been described as a bulldozer of intense, precise scholarship. He first became interested in the Synoptic Problem and the order of the pericopes in Mark, Matthew, and Luke in the late sixties. This led on to Q. By 1982, Leuven had become a center of Q studies.[14] This became the place to publish major works on Q, under Neirynck's leadership and with the help of the dynamic academic publisher Peeters. Yet Neirynck's role has not been primarily that of an exegete of Q. He began with an interest in the infancy story in the Gospel of Luke. From there he moved to technical books, like the one on duality in Mark, to explain how Mark's writing style can be explained better by his redactional habits than by the view that he is conflating Matthew and Luke (Farmer's view).[15] Another monograph is on the "minor agreements," a major problem for the two-source theory.[16] Because of his rigorous mastery of detail, Neirynck became the man to go to for short, clear statements on the Synoptic Problem and Q in widely used reference works.[17] His detailed contributions are collected in three volumes of his essays.[18] He also made a powerful contribution to the restoration of the patristic view that the Evangelist John knew and used all three of the Synoptic Gospels. (This does not exclude John's additional possession of independent early historical tradition.) Thus Neirynck's main contribution has been toward the consolidation of the two-source solution in the understanding of the entire gospel tradition. His style made enemies, but even the enemies were grateful for the detailed attention he paid them (for example, M.-E. Boismard, who received a book-length review of his own theory).

Schillebeeckx

After a youthful run-in with the censors, Neirynk avoided the commentary and theological genres within biblical studies. It was thus left to Edward Schillebeeckx (1914–2009), a Flemish Dominican, but associated for most of his life with Nijmegen, the Catholic university of the Netherlands, to work out a systematic theological synthesis where Q would show its worth. As a product of the Flemish Catholic revival in his youth, Schillebeeckx insisted on writing and publishing his works in Dutch. Once he was recognized as a rising star, his works were mostly translated into the main European languages. Among the major theologians at the Second Vatican Council, he was young enough to undertake a major project after the crisis years 1968 to 69. His great trilogy is

called in English: *Jesus, Christ, Church*.[19] Schillebeeckx was trained
as a classic Thomist in theology. But in Paris he learned a historical-critical approach to Thomas Aquinas (from M.-D. Chenu). He
also learned to appreciate and use modern philosophy, especially
phenomenological reflection.

From a biblical point of view, Schillebeeckx's most valuable
contribution is to renew Christology by using four categories for
four early gospel types. These four gospel types then express four
different Christologies and four different ecclesiologies:

- *Logoi sophon*, or words of the wise, like Q. Its domi-
  nant Christology has Jesus as Wisdom, and its ecclesiology is a Christian school or gnostic coterie.
- **Aretology**, or a collection of miracle stories. Its
  Christology presents Jesus as a divine man/hero
  type like Hercules or Elijah, and its ecclesiology as a
  healing shrine or prayer group.
- **Apocalypses**, like Mark 13 or the Book of Revelation. In its Christology Jesus is Son of Man and End-
  time Judge, and the community is an angry sect.
- **Kerygmatic gospels**, like Mark or Peter. This Christology ends with, or concentrates exclusively on, the
  death and resurrection of Jesus as saving lord; the
  community is a church for all peoples, especially
  sinners.

It is sometimes said that only the Easter kerygma can find a
church for all people and all types of people. Even if this cannot be
proven absolutely, the fact is that our four canonical Gospels each
have a passion and resurrection narrative at the end. This fact
makes our four Gospels fit well with the basic creeds of the
church, the Nicene and the Apostles'.

Although Schillebeeckx was several times tried and heard in
Rome, he escaped formal condemnation. The aspect of his work
that was most displeasing to the authorities was not, however, his

Christology but rather his writings on ministry, which do not concern us here. Rome's only serious criticism of his Christology was rather technical, not certainly valid, and in any case not directly about the Bible. Schillebeeckx is trying to do justice to the fact that, when we read the Gospels, we have the impression that we are dealing with a human person who had a unique relationship to the divine, and whom it seems appropriate to address with divine titles. Schillebeeckx wants to reject the Byzantine theology that in Christ there are two natures, human and divine, but only one divine person, and that Jesus was not therefore a human person (*anhypostasis*). Schillebeeckx prefers to affirm that Jesus is a divine person in one sense, and a human person in a later, modern sense of person as a center of consciousness. This human person exists within the divine person of the Son of God (*enhypostasis*). This view was condemned in the sixth century, but should it be today? The concept of person has developed. Schillebeeckx is trying to put the tradition into dialogue with conceptual developments.

So too in his use of Q, he is trying to explore biblical models for Christian faith and life today. First he offers a brief presentation of his basic hypothesis.[20] Then he presents a sketch of the Christological potential of a *logoi sophon*, or Wisdom Christology. In this model Jesus is servant of God, bringer-revealer-teacher of Wisdom; he is in some texts preexistent, incarnate, humbled yet exalted Wisdom. Schillebeeckx rapidly traces the evolution of this theme in the ancient Near East, especially in the Maat and Isis cults in Egypt, and then traces the reception of these cults in a cleansed form as seen in the Hebrew Bible (Prov 8 and 9; Job 28; Sirach 24). He shows the fusion of wisdom literature and apocalyptic prophecy in Daniel, which was achieved by the Jewish Pietists who eventually formed the Pharisaic and Essene parties. He then passes to the New Testament. Here he sets Q's Christology in the larger context of the New Testament Christological hymns (e.g., Phil 2:6–11; Col 1:12–20; John 1:1–18), with their dynamic movement of descent, rejection, ascent, and reign in glory, stating:

In the later phase of the Q community Jesus is associated with a pre-existent Wisdom; the latter sends her messengers, the prophets, but also the eschatological prophet, without Jesus ever being identified with pre-existent Wisdom—a circumspect Wisdom Christology. Jesus, the earthly son of man, is the Son known only by the Father because the Father has given him all authority and power, so that in him the heavenly Wisdom has come to dwell; he appears and acts as the eschatological emissary of a pre-existent Wisdom. Formulae that suggest a "sending forth" are a typical feature of this Wisdom Christology. The Matthean gospel goes further [than Q] and identifies Jesus with Wisdom; eventually, in the apocryphal *Gospel of Thomas*, Jesus identifies himself with this Wisdom.[21]

Jesus quite clearly made use of "Wisdom" sayings and proverbs. In that sense it is historically legitimate to see Jesus as a teacher of wisdom. The continuity is shown in the way the disciples emulate Jesus: just as Jesus is a mystagogue initiating people into God's secrets, so too are the apostles mystagogues. In essence, what it implies is a belief that Jesus has a connection with God and presents the question of God: he tells us about the Father.[22]

We perceive here a genuine, prudent use of Q in a larger framework to work out a Wisdom Christology. This rich balance is characteristic of Schillebeeckx.

Text Study: Judgment and Wisdom in Q

"Therefore also...Wisdom said: I will send them prophets and sages, and some of them they will kill and persecute, so that a settling of accounts for the blood of all the prophets poured out from the beginning of the world may be required of this generation, from the blood of Abel to the blood of Zechariah, murdered between the altar and the House. Yes, I tell you: An accounting will be required of this generation." (Q 11:49–51; Matt 23:34–36)

"The queen of the South will be raised at the judgment with this generation and condemn it, for she came from the ends of the earth to listen to the wisdom of Solomon, and look, something more than Solomon is here! Ninevite men will arise at the judgment with this generation and condemn it. For they repented at the announcement of Jonah, and look, something more than Jonah is here!" (Q 11:31–32; Matt 12:42, 41)

Whether these sayings go back to the historical, earthly Jesus or not, the reader can notice and learn how Q emphasizes a judgment coming in the very near future: *this generation*. The idea of judgment is expressed in the less usual language of "a settling of accounts...an accounting will be required." The biblical background is the Deuteronomistic idea of the violent end of the prophets. That is why prophets are mentioned. But so are sages, wise people. And the whole section itself is spoken by Wisdom personified. Priests are also implied in the mention of being between altar and House (a Palestinian expression for the Temple in Jerusalem). In the second excerpt, from Q 11:31–32, among the sages is the Queen of Sheba, the queen of the South; she who sought religious wisdom from Solomon, son of David, and his successor (the story is told in 1 Kings 10). Jonah is reckoned a prophet and preacher. The language of judgment and condemnation uses the more usual Greek *krisis* and *katakrinomai*, and the judgment is of this *present* generation, so it is coming soon.

These sayings are an illustration of how the earliest Christian tradition employs a fusion of ancient Israelite conceptual frameworks into a living synthesis: kings, queens, prophets, and wise men and women—all in a framework of apocalyptic eschatology with urgent immediacy. To try to disentangle what the sayings combine is undoubtedly a mistake.

The sayings presuppose that God is acting at the present time, sending various kinds of emissaries, but especially Jesus. He is elsewhere called "son of David," which probably means that he is a new and better Solomon. Solomon was a wise and good king, whose name means "peace" and who pursued a long reign of peace. To that extent Jesus is close to Solomon by his teaching of nonviolence and reconciliation. But the biblical recollection of Solomon mentions some of his flaws at the end of the account (1 Kgs 11). These flaws are not repeated by Jesus; therefore, he is greater than Solomon.

The reader is left with a difficult decision as to the "authorship" of the sayings. That Jesus had elevated states of consciousness is not doubtful; that he felt close to the wisdom of God is also not in doubt. But did he himself formulate these statements of end-time warning and appeals to repentance? That is indeed possible, perhaps even probable. It is also possible that here we find the echo of the disappointed reaction of the first disciples whom Jesus had sent out before his violent death and who continued that mission after his death. His own violent end is hinted at here too, but not its atoning significance. So Q has an awareness of that violent end, even if it does not possess the full narrative of the suffering and death of Jesus, or express a theory about the significance of that death. The reader has much to ponder in these verses; for example, why is Lady Wisdom the speaker in the first sayings?

5
THE STUDY OF Q IN NORTH AMERICA

J. M. Robinson

The more advanced study of Q in North America has been led by James McConkey Robinson and by John S. Kloppenborg. Professor Robinson was born 1924 in South Carolina, raised a member of the old Southern Presbyterian Church, studied in Marburg under Bultmann, and taught at the Southern California School of Theology and at Claremont Graduate School near Los Angeles until his retirement. He has been a leader in introducing Bultmann's approaches to the New Testament into North America. Robinson's contribution to Q studies began with an essay he wrote for the collected essays in honor of Bultmann on the occasion of his eightieth birthday.[1] The essay is entitled "*Logoi Sophon*: On the *Gattung* of Q." As we have already seen, *logoi sophon* refers to collections of wise sayings; *Gattung* is the German word for "literary genre." With this essay Robinson inaugurates a more literary-historical approach to Q. But before we address the essay in detail, we should mention a more dramatic side of his contributions.

There is a certain American optimistic attitude in biblical studies: an attitude that we can just go out into the field and dig up the answers to our biblical questions. This can-do spirit is illustrated by the Indiana Jones films that began with *Raiders of the Lost Ark*. Robinson became a kind of Indiana Jones. It had long been a scandal of international scholarship that thirteen remarkable early Christian codices (containing forty different short works), found in a sealed pot in a cemetery in Egypt at Pbou near Nag Hammadi, had been sitting rotting in the Coptic library in Cairo since their discovery in 1946, because no one could figure out a way to get the Egyptian authorities to release the texts for publication and study. (The main exception to this was the *Gospel of Thomas*, which we have already mentioned, the most important text for gospel study.) With his Southern charm, Robinson was able to raise the money necessary to pay the local officials to release the documents to him for publication.

Robinson then had an even greater adventure trying to pin down the exact location and circumstances of the discovery. Suspicious peasants were reluctant to reveal the spot, because the codices had been found in a cemetery building where villagers caught in a feud were hiding to avoid being punished for a murder. They had found them by accident. They had burned some of the codices to keep warm before someone told them they could sell for a good price on the antiquities market in Cairo. The Western world heard of the codices by 1946, a year before the discovery of the Dead Sea Scrolls. Robinson succeeded not only in getting the texts released for publication, but also in organizing an international and interconfessional team of scholars to edit and comment on the texts.[2]

Robinson was not only an academic scholar. He also wrote a short biography of Jesus in which he tells about his discoveries in the field and what they mean to him personally as a modern believer.[3] In this little book he reproduces the text of Q, but his portrait of Jesus draws on other parts of the New Testament as well. He also states several times that the Q community developed into the church of Matthew. I think this is correct.

Excursus on the *Gospel of Thomas*

The *Gospel of Thomas* is an early Christian text that contains 114 sayings attributed to the living (risen?) Jesus. Fragments exist in the gospel's original Greek, while the complete text exists in Coptic, with many Greek loan words. Many of the sayings resemble what we know from the canonical Gospels. Some sayings are, however, quite original. My personal favorites are Saying 12 (James is the first pope, not Peter), and Saying 13 (salvation comes through being illumined, and thus divinized, by Jesus). This latter point is often referred to as a Gnostic doctrine of salvation, but this leads to a debate on Gnosticism.

The great debate has been whether *Thomas* depends upon the four canonical Gospels and thus has no value as an independent witness to the historical Jesus, or whether it does have value as an independent witness. The first of these two options was favored until recently. One could say the debate had reached a stalemate.

April D. DeConick of Rice University has helped us out of this impasse somewhat. She argues that *Thomas* was a "rolling corpus" that had four layers of tradition in itself. The kernel dates from AD 30 to 50 and is apocalyptic in message. The second layer is concerned with leadership (Sayings 12 and 68.2), and dates from AD 50 to 60. The third exchanges the apocalyptic eschatology for a mystical one (Sayings 3, 18, 37, 51, 52, and 53), and dates from AD 60 to 100. The fourth layer is ascetical and has a doctrine of salvation similar to Hermetic literature; it dates from AD 80 to 120. Overall, the kernel and the fourth layer predominate. *Thomas* is a "repository of communal memory." The Gospel According to John directly attacks the mystical, visionary way to salvation promoted in *Thomas*. Both evangelists John and Thomas knew the Synoptic Gospels. DeConick does not solve the problem of the *Gospel of Thomas*'s independent historical value for research on the life of Jesus.[4]

Thomas resembles Q in genre as a collection of sayings, but it is even less structured than Q. However, its existence as just a collection of sayings supports the plausibility of the existence of Q.

Robinson's essay "*Logoi Sophon*," already mentioned, begins with an important idea. He thinks we can track the trajectory of the sayings genre, which includes such writings as the Book of Sirach and Q (especially Matthew 23:37–39 // Luke 13:34–35; that is, Jesus' lament over Jerusalem), and on to esoteric Gnostic texts ("secret sayings"), such as we find in Nag Hammadi. Beyond the literary or genre issue, however, Robinson is interested in a Christology. In the rest of the essay, he treats first the Nag Hammadi library, where he studies especially the titles of the works and of the teacher or revealer. Then he surveys the parallels in early Christian works like the *Didache*, *Pseudo-Barnabas*, and the canonical Matthew, Luke, and Mark. Next he looks at other early Christian collections of sayings of Jesus (*Herrnwort*, or dominical sayings), as found in *First Clement*; in the writings of Polycarp, Marcion, and Justin Martyr; and in the *Gospel of Thomas*. Finally he looks at Jewish wisdom literature like *Pirqe Aboth*, the *Testaments of the Twelve Patriarchs*, the *Apocalypse of Adam*, and *Ethiopic Enoch* (that is, *First Enoch*), as well as in other wisdom literature, such as the Egyptian *Instruction of Amenemope*, and the Assyrian *Words of Ahiqar*. Robinson is also interested in Matthew 23:37–39 because there Jesus uses feminine imagery to describe his maternal affection for Jerusalem. Robinson thinks that this imagery presupposes the Gnostic myth of Lady Wisdom: she comes down from heaven to enlighten suffering mankind, is often rejected, and returns to her heavenly abode. This may be true but it is not certain that it was a well worked-out pattern of salvation before the Gospel of John. (We will return to Robinson when we treat the International Q Project.)

Kloppenborg

The second main leader of Q studies in North America is John S. Kloppenborg of Toronto (born 1951). Kloppenborg built on Robinson's essay in his first book, *The Formation of Q: Trajectories in Ancient Wisdom Collections.*[5] Both Helmut Koester and J. M. Robinson influenced him in the use of the term *trajectory*. The term *wisdom collection* is also important because Kloppenborg's emphasis on the wisdom genre led him at first to downplay the aspect of prophecy, apocalyptic, and judgment in Q. This led to a lively debate. His critics felt that he gave us a Canadian Christ: extremely polite and nice, but bland, without the apocalyptic fire we find in many Q sayings. Put differently, Kloppenborg is interested in studying the morphology of a genre and this he does extremely well, with great precision and thoroughness. But when he tries to draw conclusions as to content from the constraints of the genre as such, many critics balk. He is working in the tradition of form criticism, but the formalist aspects, many think, cannot be so immediately used to draw historical conclusions, or conclusions about what can or cannot be contained within the genre, especially one as loose as that of a wisdom collection. That is why some prefer to say that Q is unique, or that it is a sayings collection, without the implication that everything must be sapiential in its content.

After this debut, Kloppenborg continued to produce a series of practical helps for people who want to study Q on their own, for example, his book *Q Parallels.*[6] Another example is an anthology of classic essays, many translated into English, on Q.[7] The high point of his practical helps is his magisterial book *Excavating Q: The History and Setting of the Sayings Gospel.*[8] Here he treats just about every aspect of the Q discussion: the history of its research, its composition and genre, its social history and geography, its theology and ideology, and the thesis of the Cynic Jesus (*Cynic* refers here to the sect of ancient Greek philosophers). The thesis of the Cynic Jesus arose because, when one reads book 3 of Epictetus's *Discourses*, one is struck by resemblances between Jesus' rules for his disciples in Q and the Stoic philosopher's presentation of Diogenes the Cynic's instruction to his disciples. There are similarities of lifestyle, but there is also a big difference in the doctrine: Diogenes does not speak about the kingdom of God, nor does he speak as an apocalyptic prophet.

This present little book owes much to Kloppenborg's synthesis. (In Jerusalem I was able to discuss his project with him as he was working on it and perhaps contributed a little bit.) Since then he has produced another introduction to Q with its text included (*The Earliest Gospel*).[9] The reader will notice his use of the term *gospel* to refer to Q in the titles of both of these works. To elevate the dignity of this document to which he has devoted so much energy, he wants to call it a gospel on the grounds that less worthy texts such as the Coptic gospels of *Thomas, Philip*, and *Truth* all bear the title. Another point to notice is that Kloppenborg insists that Q is a document with its own integrity and its own tradition history (early, middle, and late layers), in which the wisdom material is primordial and determinative. This is just the reverse of what Siegfried Schulz had decided: first apocalyptic, then wisdom. Many do not follow him in these theses. But they do affect the contemporary discussion.

The International Q Project

Seventy years ago Britain's Burnett Hillman Streeter warned that one should not try to reconstruct Q in detail, its exact wording. Whether rightly or wrongly, some of the members of the West Coast–based Jesus Seminar, after completing its group project of voting on which parts of the Gospels were more likely to go back to the historical Jesus, decided to join European colleagues in an attempt to reconstruct Q in order to produce a critical edition of it. The general editors were J. M. Robinson, Paul Hoffmann, and J. S. Kloppenborg. The group met over several years and produced a series of volumes to show their results as they progressed.[10] Then came the moment when they could present their conclusions together in an imposing deluxe volume (2000).[11] This complete work includes the Gospels of Matthew and Luke, Mark and *Thomas*, with English, German, and French translations of Q and *Thomas*. The text is divided into 101 short sections, with Q's verses printed in the order in which they are found in Luke, and concluding with Jesus' beautiful promise to his disciples: "You who have followed me will sit on thrones judging the twelve tribes of Israel." That is a nice way to end a collection of Jesus' sayings, or even more, a sayings gospel. The text of Q decided on by the committee is printed at the bottom of the page, not only in Greek, but also in English, German, and French. One can say that this is a book for scholars, but it has been mined for more popular presentations in different languages, and the three editors have done their own presentations in English and German.[12]

This magnificent production has, of course, been criticized. First of all, the title is too bold: *The Critical Edition*. It should be *A Critical Edition*. The reconstructed text is only *one* possibility. To arrive at it, many decisions had to be made, and they were always debatable. The committee itself even changed its text several times. For example, the committee at first thought that Q contained no account of the baptism of Jesus. Now it is back in, tersely, with the words "*was baptized…Spirit…Son.*" Fragmentary, but there.

To these criticisms, the committee can answer that two heads are better than one, that they have done their work in the open as a team, and that they have tried to explain and justify their decisions. More than that one could hardly ask. It is up to the users to realize the limitations and the dangers.

In near despair of stopping the Q juggernaut, Britain's anti-Q Michael Goulder made one more fierce attack shortly before his death. In it he argues that the method employed by the International Q Project is self-contradictory. It retains what in Q differs from normal or redactional or typical Matthew. However, Goulder argues, even when this is done, Q still remains close to Matthew. Therefore, there is no need for Q at all. Luke got it all from Matthew. Kloppenborg replies that, as distinct from Matthew's theology, Q also has three unique emphases: (1) a Deuteronomic theology of history, (2) a Lot cycle, and (3) an interest in Sophia, Lady Wisdom. This is interesting and worth thinking about, but even the reader sympathetic to Q wonders whether Matthew does not have a Deuteronomistic theology of his own.[13]

In this battle of the titans, I feel like I am watching two buffalo on a prairie charging each other head-on. When they collide, the whole prairie shakes.

Returning to the International Q Project, we should mention that it is producing a series of volumes titled Documenta Q (around thirty when completed) on small units of Q. For each passage, a database author reviews journal articles, monographs, and commentaries[14] since 1863 that have applied the two-source hypothesis, as listed in the bibliography included in each volume (1863 being the date of Holtzmann's study of the Synoptic Gospels that gained Q general acceptance). Wherever Matthew and Luke disagree in placement or wording, scholarly opinion is presented in four sections: arguments that Luke preserves Q, that Luke does not preserve Q, that Matthew preserves Q, and that Matthew does not preserve Q. The database author as well as several additional evaluators make a judgment call on each variant as to which version is more likely Q, give reasons for their choices, and rate how confident they are in it by assigning a letter from A, meaning virtual certainty, to D, meaning slight inclination. This is a complex procedure. Not everyone has the patience to work through this careful accumulation of material. Despite the immense labors expended, certainty in the results is not to be expected. But the arguments are there.

U.S. Catholics: Brown, Fitzmyer, and Meier

In our report on the North American reception of Q, we will now take a quick glance at three of the major American Catholic masters of gospel study: Brown, Fitzmyer, and Meier. The Sulpician priest Raymond E. Brown (1928–98) was best known for his work on the Gospel of John, but he also worked on the infancy stories of Matthew and Luke and on the passion narratives of all four Gospels. These works did not require him to take a stand on Q. However, before his much-regretted death, he published a thorough introduction to the New Testament in which he treats the Synoptic Problem and Q in a spirit close to what we have been presenting as the mainstream.[15]

More deeply involved is the two-volume commentary on Luke by the Jesuit Joseph Fitzmyer (b. 1920).[16] This great work is characterized by a tough-minded balance. In the introduction he offers arguments against Luke's direct knowledge of Matthew, and in favor of Luke's use of Mark and Q. Luke's famous fear of doublets does not prevent him from preserving thirty Marcan-Q overlaps, to the great joy of historians.

From the next generation of Q scholars comes Father John P. Meier (b. 1942), who undertook a five-volume study of the historical Jesus, under the puzzling title *A Marginal Jew*.[17] In his consideration of sources for such a study he briefly states that he accepts the standard two-source hypothesis, including Q, both because his own study of Matthew has made it seem the best founded, and because it is the most widely used in international scholarship, and this even though he is perfectly well aware of the problems and alternatives. (In fact, he does not give much attention to Goulder-Goodacre, but considers W. Farmer the main alternative.) Farmer's steady effort over a lifetime to overturn the two-source theory in favor of Mark abbreviating Matthew and Luke seems to have failed. As one of its supporters, David Dungan, said to me: The neo-Griesbach hypothesis (as Farmer's view is often called) is not for the faint of heart.[18] In his second volume, Meier has a further treatment, an excursus on the Q Document, where the by-now-famous mantra occurs: "Q is a hypothetical document whose exact extension, wording, originating community, strata, and stages of redaction cannot be known."[19]

Although Irish-born John Dominic Crossan has moved beyond his earlier positions now, one of his contributions should be mentioned. At his best Crossan has a strong sense of literary, even poetic, form. That is why he began as a student of the para-

bles. In regard to Q and similar texts, perhaps his most important
contribution is work of 1983: *In Fragments: The Aphorisms of
Jesus.*[20] Since the sayings source Q can be in large measure understood as a collection of aphorisms, Crossan's analytical form criticism of the genre, which goes beyond Bultmann in finesse, is a
contribution to the study of Q, even if he includes aphorisms from
Thomas and other parts of the Jesus tradition. In this book he does
not make detailed historical claims. He rather emphasizes the role
of oral performance and says that the short written texts were to
be expanded in performance, not simply memorized and repeated
word for word. What persists in the variations is the structure
(*ipsissima structura*). These performance variations are to be dis-
tinguished from hermeneutical and translational variants.

U.S. Protestants: Davies, Allison, and Perrin

Among Protestants working in America, the Welsh-born
W. D. Davies (1911–2001), my beloved thesis advisor, collabo-
rated with his brilliant doctoral student Dale C. Allison (b. 1955)
to produce a major commentary on Matthew in three volumes.[21]
In the introduction they discuss Q as a hypothesis they accept and
then answer some of the usual objections. Allison has also written
two works on Q, one a series of studies of the Jesus tradition in Q,
the other a study of the use of the Old Testament in Q. He has then
gone on to write three works on the life of Jesus, wherein he
strongly maintains the view of Jesus as a millenarian prophet.[22]
Allison may not always be right, but he usually is superior to his
critics, because he is less shy about historical messiness.

English-born Norman Perrin (1920–1976) wrote a practical
introduction to the New Testament in which Q is treated in the
chapter on apocalyptic Christianity.[23] He notes that the Son of
man is so important for Q that Jesus as the Son is not only coming
in the future to judge, but Jesus is also the Son of man in his
earthly ministry. I mention these authors as representative of

Protestant scholars. There are too many other examples to mention them all.

Mack and Fleddermann

The California-based scholar Burton Lee Mack, after failing to have the reception he had hoped for in his radical book on Mark, decided to write a more popular book on Q. It is entitled *The Lost Gospel: The Book of Q and Christian Origins.*[24] His work is representative of the more radical wing of Q studies, which would include J. D. Crossan as well, but whom we will not be able to discuss in detail.[25]

Mack first tells the story of the nineteenth-century recognition of Q. He then offers his own reconstruction of Q in English. But he does this twice. The first time he gives only what he thinks is the earliest (and therefore best) layer of Q, the sapiential. He then presents the whole of Q. The later layers are less to his liking. His romantic presuppositions here emerge clearly. He wants a dreamy early Christianity, free from dogma, morals, church structure, and rules. His gospel is politically correct and appropriately liberated. He is quite lucid and honest about it: if you take Q as it exists in the Synoptics in the double tradition, it is still too orthodox, too apocalyptic, too judgmental, too ethical, and too Jewish to suit his book. (One side benefit of his book is this: He wrote his dissertation in German and published it so in 1973. It is on wisdom in Philo and the New Testament and he did a fine job. It is here summarized on pages 149 to 159.)

For Mack, Jesus is a sage in the asocial, iconoclastic tradition of the ancient Cynics. Instead of a church, there were Q people. The kingdom is interpreted as the sovereign bearing of the disciple who is superior to all the conventions and demands of society. Everything is highly individualistic. There is no place for Jesus' suffering, dying, and rising for the salvation of the people. Mack's book becomes repetitive, churning, thrashing, obsessed with myth; he is puzzled by how the original Jesus' message could have been replaced by a Christ myth. In the book Jesus disappears. There is no clear personal stand. It is weak in thought. The book's historical reconstruction is a sociological fantasy.

The most extraordinary American work on Q is perhaps the long, thorough commentary by H. T. Fleddermann.[26] He adopts some positions that many find extreme. He thinks of Q as a perfectly structured and delimited work, possessing a real literary unity coming from a single author with a precise literary and theological project. His Q contains not the generally accepted 220 or so verses but 453. His criteria for what to include are primarily literary and aesthetic: chiasms, hook words, intentional repetitions, and parallelisms. He is convinced of Q's philosophical, human, literary, and theological excellence.[27] For him, Q is a gospel.

Fleddermann's remarkable industry has been rewarded with some reservations by critics, who regret his decision to assume that Mark knew Q and to depend upon this assumption in the overlaps.[28] This idea is a third-degree hypothesis that is very hard to prove. Here I refer once again to my own study of the overlaps (mentioned in chapter 1), which convince me that Q and Mark are each echoing, independently of one another, the same teaching of Jesus, as recorded by two early independent witnesses. Using Fleddermann's view, the criterion of multiple attestation would shrink in its applicability. It will take some time to assess the helpfulness of Fleddermann's work.

Recent Developments

In 2006, the four universities of western (French-speaking) Switzerland held a colloquium in Geneva and Lausanne on Q studies as they had progressed to that point. The published collection of twelve contributors gives a good idea of the state of research.[29] To mention some of the contributors: John S. Kloppenborg and Migaku Sato addressed Q as wisdom and prophecy.

Thomas Schmeller concentrated on the socio-historical context, the bearers of the Q traditions, and the audience for whom the collection was intended. A.-J. Levine treated women in Q. Ulrich Luz and Christoph Heil treated the reception of Q in Matthew and Luke respectively. Jens Schroeter added nuance to the use of Q researching the historical Jesus. In my experience of the conference, the strongest paper was by Joseph Verheyden of Leuven on the central role of the judgment of Israel in Q.

Around the same time appeared James D. G. Dunn's book supporting the idea that Q does not contain a passion narrative because it represents a tradition that began *during* the public ministry of Jesus in Galilee, before the crucifixion happened. Dunn wants to explain Q as first an oral tradition, before it was written down. He admits that some think of the Q tradition as having begun as shorthand notes, which to me is probable. But he argues for a perduring oral tradition. It would be unwise to deny that there was oral tradition in early Christianity. But since oral tradition is "uncontrollable" as a historical source, most scholars still prefer to think in terms of written sources. This preference for written sources goes back to the rules for medieval university debates. How else could the judges decide? The preference was then taken up by the Protestant Reformers. Even if one admits the existence of oral tradition, one should be aware that it is a formula easy to abuse. We must remain grateful to the scholastics and the Reformers for their efforts to call us to biblical, textual, and public sources and responsibility.[30]

More recent is the research of a young Italian at Harvard, Giovanni Battista Bazzano. He has done original work on the phenomenon of bilingual (Coptic-Greek) village scribes in Egypt in the early Christian centuries.[31] This research is important in order to continue the belief that the author of Q was a direct hearer of Jesus who took down notes from his preaching and teaching. We assume that Jesus spoke in Aramaic, so with the newer views of Q as a Greek document, it is important to realize that there were such bilingual scribes in Galilee, connected with tax-collecting, among other occupations. Galilee was about half Greek-speaking and half Aramaic-speaking at the time of Jesus, if we go by the inscriptions found there. Such experiences of bilingualism back then may seem far-fetched to us, even though today they are an everyday experience—for example, in classrooms where English-speaking teachers lecture to students who take notes in Spanish. And in the not-so-distant past, theology professors lectured in Latin (in Chicago!), and the students took notes in English. Such bilingual experiences are even more common in Europe. Ask a Swiss shopkeeper. My own explorations in this area have been published by Eve-Marie Becker and Anders Runnesson in their second volume of studies on Mark and Matthew.[32]

It is obvious that Q is a lively area of research within New Testament studies, even though it is often surrounded by controversy and skepticism. Q fascinates because it is short and manageable. It is not monochromatic but contains a variety of theological traditions and accents. It represents a layer of early Jesus material, and it balances other aspects of biblical faith. With all due methodological caution, it supports the quest of the woman with a flow of blood who wants to lay hold of the hem of Jesus' garment and so receive his healing power. Like other parts of Scripture, it can be used and abused; it can be used to nourish or to harm Christian faith. Read and cherished as a part of a larger whole, it can be of help in focusing on some early authentic elements of the Jesus tradition. More than that, there is no need to ask.

What would a spirituality of Q look like? The present author would not presume to answer that for others. Spirituality is the personal side of faith, or represents a personal appropriation of faith. Still, one can recommend that the reader take the text of Q, in whatever form is available, and quietly meditate on the sayings over several days. Ask: What sort of man speaks like that? Who is he? How much of what he says can I receive and appropriate in my own life and faith and prayer?

Text Study: Q's Final Verses

"You who have followed me will sit…on thrones judging the twelve tribes of Israel." (Q 22:28, 30)

This end-time promise of reward, power, and royal status concludes the document Q in most reconstructions. This is so because it comes last in the double tradition, shared by Matthew and Luke. It is in many ways a fitting conclusion because it fits with the centrality of the judgment theme in Q. As with the promise of the kingdom of God as something good and desirable, it offers a positive message of hope to those who follow Jesus.

Our reconstructed Q follows Luke, who does not say "twelve thrones," but only "twelve tribes." The words *twelve tribes* in the language of the Bible means all Israel, and further, the whole people of God. The disciples in this Q form, those who follow Jesus, are thus not limited to the Twelve. The judging will occur in the future, when the kingdom of God comes in its fullness. The plural *thrones* is probably inspired by the thrones in Daniel 7:9. The word *judging* means, as it often does in the Bible, "governing" in all of its different aspects, not just judging cases. Although Q does not mention the Son of man here, the Danielic background and the role of the Son of man elsewhere in Q suggests that the disciples will share this judging function with him.

This saying forms a fitting ending to Q, if there ever was one. There is a certain tension between this saying and the teaching on humility (e.g., Matt 20:20–28), but it is not insurmountable. Has the reader ever thought of him- or herself as fitting as into the role of an end-time coregent? Probably not, but this final verse in Q promises this exalted status to Jesus' followers. As Pope Leo the Great said in a Christmas sermon: "Christians, be aware of your dignity."

CONCLUSION

Our little survey has tried to give a mostly chronological report on the scholarly study of Q, the sayings source of the teachings of Jesus, in the last two centuries, and especially the recent discussion about Q on two continents, Europe and North America, and among different confessions and languages.

We conclude this book in terms of Aristotle's four questions:

1. *An sit?* Does Q exist?—for Q's very existence is still a debated issue.
2. *Quid sit?* What is Q?—the search for a definition.
3. *Quomodo sit?* How do we know about Q?
4. *Propter quid? Quare?* Why does Q exist?—that is, Why should we care about Q? What good purpose does it serve?

These questions have all been treated in this survey and are briefly summed up here. To be sure, the answers cannot always be neatly separated. The questions overlap a bit.

1. Does Q exist? Except for a noisy faction in Britain and France that still resists this conclusion, it is highly probable that Q exists, meaning that it existed for a brief time (ca 40–50 years) as a collection of sayings, a few attributed to the Baptist but most to Jesus. Once its contents had been incorporated into the two longer Synoptic Gospels, Matthew and Luke, it disappeared as a separate collection around AD 90.

2. What is Q? Q is the material that was found to be common to Matthew and Luke, once their use of Mark as a common base narrative had been recognized, but which is not present in Mark itself. It happens that most of this common material consists of sayings of Jesus, but there are a few narratives, such as the three temptations of Jesus and the centurion's boy. This material strikes the reader as early Palestinian tradition, marked by apocalyptic hope for a just future with punishment for the wicked, fused with an interest in divinely revealed wisdom about how to live and how to triumph in the final judgment.

3. How do we know about Q? We know about Q through a study of the Gospels read in synoptic parallel columns. The document is the result of a scholarly hypothesis developed to explain this common material, roughly 220 verses, and this hypothesis depends on a prior hypothesis, that Mark is the earliest Gospel preserved as an independent whole. Q seems, however, to have been written earlier than Mark. It is often dated between AD 40 and 70, in Southern Syria or Northern Roman Palestine.

4. Why should we care about Q? Here we will furnish two answers, a conservative and a liberal one. The conservative answer is that we are interested in Q because it gives us access to the earliest layer(s) of Jesus material and so helps us to grasp Jesus' message, his mind, his sense of himself and of his mission, his powerful hopes and promises, his stringent demands, and his warnings of judgment. The liberal answer is that we are also interested in these earliest layers where there is present an awareness of Jesus' violent end but without a developed interpretation of its meaning, such as we find in Mark 10:45.

There is a strong Christology in Q (Jesus is identified with the Son of man and is connected with personified Wisdom), but there is no use of the title Christ. So we have a paradoxical situation, a Christology without a Christ. The liberal view is interested also in the "Q people," the communities that preserved and tried to live by these teachings of Jesus. So we have another paradox, an ecclesiology without the term *church*. Both the conservative and the liberal approaches can teach us something about earliest Christianity. My personal criteria to evaluate modern lives of Jesus based primarily on Q is this: "How much of Q can they not stomach? How much of Q must they jettison or leave out, in order to construct their modernized picture?" These are signs of weakness, both historical and theological. Like anything else, Q can be put to many different purposes, some good, some bad.

My hope for the reader is that he or she will now possess an edition of Q such as that provided by J. M. Robinson (thirty-five pages, a pamphlet), and slowly meditate on each of the sayings, asking such questions as I suggested before: What sort of person is speaking in these sayings? Are these sayings meaningful for my life? If so, how? Is this the master of wisdom about life and the divine plan for the human future whom I wish to follow? What is missing in this picture (that needs to be supplemented by the other books of the New Testament)? Do I want to take only part, not the whole package, of Q?

St. Ignatius of Loyola did something similar to modern editions of Q when he provided, in his *Spiritual Exercises*, thirty extracts from the Gospels to be meditated on during the thirty days of a retreat.

NOTES

1. Introduction

1. J. S. Kloppenborg, *The Formation of Q: Trajectories in Ancient Wisdom Collections* (Philadelphia: Fortress, 1987), 329–41. This offers a long list, from Egypt and the ancient Near East.

2. Martin Hengel, *The Four Gospels and the One Gospel of Jesus Christ* (Harrisburg, PA: Trinity Press International, 2000).

3. Birger Gerhardsson, *The Shema in the New Testament* (Lund, Sweden: Novapress, 1996), 13–23; *The Testing of God's Son* (CB NT 2:1: Lund, Sweden: Gleerup, 1966).

4. J. M. Robinson and Helmut Koester, *Trajectories through Early Christianity* (Philadelphia: Fortress, 1971).

5. J. D. Crossan, *The Historical Jesus* (San Francisco: Harper, 1991); B. L. Mack, *The Lost Gospel: The Book of Q and Christian Origins* (San Francisco: Harper, 1993).

2. The Discovery and Reception of Q in Germany

1. This sentence is found in Eusebius, *Church History*, 3:39, 16.

2. "Über die Zeugnisse von Papias von unsern beiden ersten Evangelien," *Theologische Studien und Kritiken* 4 (1832): 735–68. I am using the critical edition, Schleiermacher, *Exegetische Schriften* (Berlin: de Gruyter, 2001), 228–54. There is no complete English translation.

3. B. W. Bacon, "The Five Books of Matthew against the Jews," *The Expositor* 15 (1918): 56–66. Bacon adds the idea of a Matthean Pen-

tateuch, which Schleiermacher does not have, and Bacon expands his ideas into the long book *Studies in Matthew* (New York: Holt, 1930).

4. H. J. Holtzmann, *Die Synoptische Evangelien* (Leipzig: Engelmann, 1863).

5. A. Harnack, *The Sayings of Jesus: The Second Source of St. Matthew and St. Luke* (London: Williams and Norgate / New York: Putnam, 1908); original *Sprüche und Reden Jesu: Die zweite Quelle des Matthaeus und Lukas* (Leipzig: J. C. Hinrichs, 1907).

6. Harnack, *Sayings*, 300.

7. On Harnack, I am depending particularly on the two books by K. H. Neufeld: *Adolf von Harnack* (Paderborn: Bonifacius, 1977), and *Adolf Harnacks Konflikt mit der Kirche* (Innsbruck: Tyrolia, 1979).

8. S. Schulz, *Q: Die Spruchquelle der Evangelisten* (Zurich: Theologischer Verlag, 1972).

9. Klaus Koch, *The Rediscovery of Apocalyptic* (SBT, n.s. 22; Naperville, IL: Allenson, 1972). This tells the story of the desperate attempts to avoid or minimize apocalyptic in the Bible.

10. J. A. Fitzmyer inclines to the authenticity of Q 10:22 in his three-volume Anchor Bible Commentary on Luke (New York: Doubleday, 1985), 2:870.

11. Flusser, *Judaism and the Origins of Christianity* (Jerusalem: Magnes, 1988), 509–14.

12. Ulrich Luz, *Matthew 8–20* (Hermeneia; Minneapolis: Fortress, 2001), 158, n. 19.

13. Ibid., 166.

14. Ibid., 159, but see also all of 155–76.

15. Alfred Loisy, *Les evangiles synoptiques* (Ceffonds: chez l'auteur, 1907), 1.905–15.

16. Albert Houssiau, "L'exegese de Matthieu xi, 27b selon saint Irenee," *ETL* 29 (1953): 328–54.

17. A. Y. Collins, "The Origin of the Designation of Jesus as Son of Man," *Harvard Theological Review* 80 (1987): 391–407; J. P. Meier, in NJBC, 1324–25.

18. H. E. Todt, *The Son of Man in the Synoptic Tradition* (Philadelphia: Westminster, 1965).

19. J. J. Collins, *Daniel* (Hermeneia; Minneapolis: Fortress, 1993).

20. B. T. Viviano, "Making Sense of the Matthean Genealogy: Matthew 1:17 and the Theology of History," in Jeremy Corley, ed., *New*

Perspectives on the Nativity (London/New York: T & T Clark-Continuum, 2009), 91–109.

21. Frank Stagg, "The Abused Aorist," *JBL* 91 (1972): 222–31.

22. See Dale C. Allison, Jr., *The Intertextual Jesus: Scripture in Q* (Harrisburg, PA: Trinity Press International, 2000), 43–51.

23. G. F. Moore, *Judaism in the Tannaitic Period* (Cambridge, MA: Harvard University Press, 1927), vol. 1, 526–27; vol. 3, 161. The Babylonian Talmud: *Pesahim* 54a; *Nedarim* 39b; *Genesis Rabba* 1.4.

24. See the debate between Thorleif Boman (*Hebrew Thought Compared with Greek* [London: SCM, 1960]) and James Barr (*Old and New in Interpretation* [London: SCM, 1966]). Or see Martin Hengel, *Judaism and Hellenism* (Philadelphia: Fortress, 1974).

25. David Flusser, "Hillel's Self-Awareness and Jesus, 'I Am in the Midst of Them (Mt. 18:20),'" in his *Judaism and the Origins of Christianity* (Jerusalem: Magnes, 1988), 509–14, and 515–25. Cf. J. D. G. Dunn, *Christology in the Making* (Philadelphia: Westminster, 1980), 196–201.

3. The Reception of Q in the British Isles

1. Henning Graf Reventlow, *The Authority of the Bible and the Rise of the Modern World* (Philadelphia: Fortress, 1984).

2. Ieuan Ellis, *Seven Against Christ: A Study of "Essays and Reviews"* (Leiden: Brill, 1980).

3. B. H. Streeter, *The Four Gospels* (London & New York: Macmillan, St. Martins, 1924); B. H. Streeter, *The Primitive Church* (London: Macmillan, 1929); C. M. Tuckett, "Streeter," in *TRE* 32 (2000): 249–52; J. M. Court, "Burnett Hillman Streeter," *Expository Times* 118 (2006): 19–25.

4. Streeter, *Four Gospels*, 227.

5. Ibid., 92.

6. Stephen Neill, *The Interpretation of the New Testament 1861–1961* (London: Oxford University Press, 1964).

7. F. C. Burkitt, *The Gospel History and Its Transmission* (Edinburgh: T & T Clark, 1906; 2nd ed., 1907), 148–68.

8. The major study of the overlaps is by Rudolf Laufen, *Die Doppelueberlieferungen der Logienquelle und des Markusevangeliums* (BBB 54; Koenigstein: Peter Hanstein, 1980). I have tried to write a more mod-

est essay: "The Historical Jesus in the Doubly Attested Sayings: An Experiment," *Revue Biblique* 103 (1996): 367–410; reprinted in my *Trinity-Kingdom-Church* (NTOA 48; Göttingen: Vandenhoeck & Ruprecht, 2001), 21–63.

9. Janet Soskice, *The Sisters of Sinai: How Two Lady Adventurers Discovered the Hidden Gospels* (New York: Knopf, 2009).

10. Austin Farrer, "On Dispensing with Q," in *Studies in the Gospels in Memory of R. H. Lightfoot*, ed. Dennis E. Nineham (Oxford: Blackwell, 1955), 57–88; available online at http://www.markgoodacre. org/Q/farrer.htm.

11. M. D. Goulder, *Midrash and Lection in Matthew* (London: SPCK, 1974; repr. Eugene, OR: Wipf & Stock, 2004); *Luke: A New Paradigm*, 2 vols. (JSNTSup 20; Sheffield: JSOT, 1989); "Is Q a Juggernaut?" *JBL* 115 (1996): 667–81.

12. In his book on Matthew, Goulder may not yet have totally rejected the existence of Q. He refers to it on page 72 and onward. But on page 97, note 6, he says that Luke knew and used Matthew. Perhaps Goulder only uses Q as a shorthand way of referring to the double tradition, without implying that he thinks it was once a document on its own.

13. F. G. Downing, "A Paradigm Perplex: Luke, Matthew and Mark," *NTS* 38 (1992): 15–36; "Compositional Conventions and the Synoptic Problem," *JBL* 107 (1988): 69–85.

14. Goulder rightly says that Q is not an independent hypothesis, but rather a corollary of the two-source hypothesis.

15. The recent article by S. D. Black, "One Really Striking Minor Agreement" *NovT* 52 (2010): 313–33), is informative, clear, and balanced. It shows that all source-critical approaches stumble here, because Mark is once again so enigmatic. It concludes that while the two-source theory still remains the best solution, this particular case remains a problem. The integrity of textual criticism must be upheld.

16. Mark S. Goodacre, *The Case Against Q* (Harrisburg, PA: Trinity Press International, 2002). Goodacre also has an insightful Web site by the same name.

17. On the aesthetic turn in exegesis and its dangers, see B. T. Viviano, "The Adoration of the Magi: Matthew 2:1–23 and Theological Aesthetics," *Revue Biblique* 115 (2008): 546–67.

18. J. S. Kloppenborg, "On Dispensing with Q? Goodacre on the Relation of Luke to Matthew," *NTS* 49 (2003): 210–36, esp. 221–22.

There is another earlier, intense exchange between Goulder and C. M. Tuckett: Goulder, "On Putting Q to the Test," *NTS* 24 (1978): 218–34; Tuckett replies with "On the Relationship between Matthew and Luke," *NTS* 30 (1984): 130–42.

19. F. G. Downing, "Compositional Conventions and the Synoptic Problem," *JBL* 107 (1988): 69–85; "A Paradigm Perplex: Luke, Matthew and Mark," *NTS* 38 (1992): 15–36.

20. Francis B. Watson, "Q as Hypothesis: A Study in Methodology," *NTS* 55 (2009): 397–415.

21. Jan Lambrecht, "John the Baptist and Jesus in Mark 1.1–15: Markan Redaction of Q," *NTS* 38 (1992): 357–84. Cf. H. T. Fleddermann, *Mark and Q* (BETL 122; Leuven: University Press, 1995).

22. Birger Gerhardsson, *The Testing of God's Son* (ConNT 20; Lund, Sweden: Gleerup, 1964).

23. Watson, "Q as Hypothesis," 408, n. 24, quoting Jens Schroeter, "Die Frage nach dem historischen Jesus und der Charakter historischer Erkenntnis," in *The Sayings Source Q and the Historical Jesus*, ed. Andreas Lindemann (BETL 158; Leuven: University Press, 2001), 207–54.

24. C. M. Tuckett, *Q and the History of Early Christianity: Studies in Q* (Peabody, MA: Hendrickson; Edinburgh: T & T Clark, 1996). See S. J. Patterson, "Q and the History of Early Christianity: Studies on Q," *JBL* 117 (1998): 744–46.

25. D. R. Catchpole, *The Quest for Q* (Edinburgh: T & T Clark, 1993).

26. Catchpole, "The Centurion's Faith and Its Function in Q," in *The Four Gospels* (Neirynck Festschrift; Leuven: Peeters, 1992), 517–40.

27. Catchpole, "The Beginning of Q: A Proposal," *NTS* 38 (1992): 205–21.

28. 2DH = Two-Document Hypothesis = Two-Source Hypothesis. This is Kloppenborg's terminology. Kloppenborg does not like to say "two sources" because he does not want to say that Q is merely a source (of Matthew and Luke), but, rather, is an independent gospel in its own right.

29. C. M. Tuckett, "The Current State of the Synoptic Problem," in Paul Foster et al., *New Studies in the Synoptic Problem* (BETL 239; Leuven: Peeters, 2011), 50.

30. Richard Pervo, *The Acts of the Apostles* (Hermeneia; Minneapolis: Fortress, 2010).

31. Gilbert Highet, *The Classical Tradition* (Oxford: University Press, 1949), 499.

4. The Catholic Reception of the Q Postulate

1. Bernard Montagnes, *The Story of Father Marie-Joseph Lagrange: Founder of Modern Catholic Bible Study*, trans. Benedict Viviano (New York / Mahwah, NJ: Paulist, 2006). Earlier biographies of Lagrange and further studies by Montagnes on Lagrange are listed in this English edition.

2. M.-J. Lagrange, *Evangile selon S. Marc* (Paris: Gabalda, 1910), cxv–cxvi.

3. Kloppenborg's *Excavating Q: The History and Setting of the Sayings Gospel* (Minneapolis: Fortress, 2000), especially pages 314 to 28, gives a more complex and nuanced version of this story.

4. The decrees are available in many places, for example, *Rome and the Study of Scripture* (St. Meinrad, IN: Grail, 1962). The original languages are in *Enchiridion Biblicum*, 3rd ed. (Naples: M. D'Auria, 1956).

5. A. F. Loisy, *Les evangiles synoptiques*, 2 vols. (Ceffonds, France: Chez l'auteur, 1907–8).

6. This particular incident is described in N. M. Lahutsky, "Paris and Jerusalem: Alfred Loisy and Pere Lagrange on the Gospel of Mark," *CBQ* 52 (1990): 444–66.

7. Bruno de Solages, *Comment sont nes les evangiles Marc, Luc, Matthieu* (Toulouse: Editions Privat, 1973).

8. Josef Schmid, *Matthaeus und Lukas: Eine Untersuchung des Verhaeltnisses ihrer Evangelien* (Biblische Studien 23/2–4; Freiburg: Herder, 1930).

9. Kloppenborg, *Excavating Q*, 317, n. 100.

10. Alfred Wikenhauser, *New Testament Introduction* (New York: Herder & Herder, 1958; orig. German ed., 1953). The revised German edition of 1973 is even better.

11. Paul Hoffmann, *Studien zur Theologie der Logienquelle* (Neutestamentliche Abhandlungen, n.f., 8; Münster: Aschendorff, 1972).

12. Paul Hoffmann, *Jesus von Nazareth und die Kirche* (Stuttgart: Katholisches Bibelwerk, 2009). Here I am drawing on the review by S. Witetschek, *RBL* 6/2011.

13. The text of this document can be found in J. A. Fitzmyer, *The Interpretation of Scripture* (New York / Mahwah, NJ: Paulist, 2008), 50–58; he introduces and comments on the text in 38–50, esp. 48–50.

14. Joel Delobel, ed., *Logia* (Leuven: Peeters, 1982).

15. F. Neirynck, *Duality in Mark* (BETL 31; Leuven: University Press, 1972).

16. F. Neirynck, *The Minor Agreements of Matthew and Luke against Mark* (BETL 37; Louvain: University Press, 1974).

17. "The Synoptic Problem," in *The New Jerome Biblical Commentary*, ed. R. E. Brown et al. (Englewood Cliffs, NJ: Prentice-Hall, 1990), 587–95; articles on the Synoptic Problem and on Q, in the *Interpreter's Dictionary of the Bible*, sup. vol. (Nashville: Abingdon, 1976), 845–48 and 715–16.

18. *Evangelica* I, II, III (BETL 60, 99, 150; Leuven: Peeters, 1982, 1991, 2001).

19. E. Schillebeeckx, *Jesus* (New York: Seabury, 1979); *Christ* (New York: Seabury, 1980); *Church* (New York: Crossroad, 1990). My own evaluation of the project is in my *Trinity-Kingdom-Church* (Göttingen: Vandenhoeck, 2001), 75–87.

20. Schillebeeckx, *Jesus*, 100–102.

21. Ibid., 429–32, quotation at 430–31.

22. Ibid., 432.

5. The Study of Q in North America

1. *Zeit und Geschichte*, ed. Erich Dinkler and Hartwig Thyen (Tübingen: Mohr-Siebeck, 1964). This volume had the unusual distinction of being in great measure translated into English: *The Future of Our Religious Past*, ed. J. M. Robinson (London: SCM, 1971). Robinson's essay is found on pages 84–130 in this volume.

2. Bentley Layton, *The Gnostic Scriptures* (Anchor Bible Research Library; New York: Doubleday, 1987), xxvii. The text of the *Gospel of Thomas* is given on 376–99.

3. J. M. Robinson, *The Gospel of Jesus* (San Francisco: Harper, 2005). In the same year, Robinson's collected essays on Q were published as *The Sayings Gospel Q* (BETL 189; Leuven: Peeters, 2005).

4. April D. DeConick, *Recovering the Original Gospel of Thomas: A History of the Gospel and Its Growth* (Edinburgh: T & T Clark, 2005); Christopher W. Skinner, *What are They Saying About the Gospel of Thomas* (New York / Mahwah, NJ: Paulist, 2012).

5. J. S. Kloppenborg, *The Formation of Q: Trajectories in Ancient Wisdom Collections* (Philadelphia: Fortress, 1987).

6. J. S. Kloppenborg, *Q Parallels: Synopsis, Critical Notes & Concordance* (Sonoma, CA: Polebridge, 1988).

7. J. S. Kloppenborg, ed., *The Shape of Q: Signal Essays on the Sayings Gospel* (Minneapolis: Fortress, 1994).

8. J. S. Kloppenborg, *Excavating Q: The History and Setting of the Sayings Gospel* (Minneapolis: Fortress, 2000).

9. J. S. Kloppenborg, *The Earliest Gospel: An Introduction to the Original Stories and Sayings of Jesus* (Louisville, KY: Westminster John Knox, 2008).

10. For example, *Documenta Q: Reconstructions of Q Through Two Centuries of Gospel Research Excerpted, Sorted and Evaluated, Q 11:2b–4: The Lord's Prayer* (Leuven: Peeters, 1996). This volume was entrusted to Shawn Carruth, OSB, and Albrecht Garsky. The volume editor is S. D. Anderson.

11. James M. Robinson, Paul Hoffmann, and John S. Kloppenborg, *The Critical Edition of Q* (Minneapolis: Fortress / Leuven: Peeters, 2000).

12. For example, there is a handy and successful French edition by Frederic Amsler, *L'evangile inconnu: La source des paroles de Jesus* (Geneva: Labor et Fides, 2001).

13. M. Goulder, "Self-Contradiction in the IQP," *JBL* 118 (1999): 506–17; R. A. Derenbacker, Jr., and J. S. Kloppenborg Verbin, "Self-Contradiction in the IQP? A Reply to Michael Goulder," *JBL* 120 (2001): 57–76. On Matthew and Deuteronomy, the classic work is Hubert Frankemoelle's *Jahwe-Bund und Kirche Christi* (Münster: Aschendorff, 1984).

14. Cf. D. D. Turlington's review of two of the Documenta Q volumes in *JBL* 118 (1999): 557–58.

15. R. E. Brown, *An Introduction to the New Testament* (New York: Doubleday, 1997), 111–25.

16. J. A. Fitzmyer, *The Gospel According to Luke*, 2 vol. (Anchor Bible Commentary; New York: Doubleday, 1981, 1985), esp. 73–81.

17. J. P. Meier, *A Marginal Jew: Rethinking the Historical Jesus*, 5 vol. (New York: Doubleday, 1991).

18. W. R. Farmer, *The Synoptic Problem* (New York: Macmillan, 1964).

19. J. P. Meier, *A Marginal Jew*, vol. 2 (New York: Doubleday, 1994), 177–81; quotation on 178.

20. J. D. Crossan, *In Fragments: The Aphorisms of Jesus* (San Francisco: Harper & Row, 1983).

21. W. D. Davies and Dale C. Allison, *A Critical and Exegetical Commentary on the Gospel According to Saint Matthew* (ICC; Edinburgh: T & T Clark, 1988, 1991, 1997). Q is treated in the introduction, vol. 1, 115–21.

22. Dale C. Allison, *The Jesus Tradition in Q* (Harrisburg, PA: Trinity Press International, 1997); *The Intertextual Jesus: Scripture in Q* (Harrisburg, PA: Trinity Press International, 2000); plus three studies of the historical Jesus where Q figures prominently: *Jesus of Nazareth: Millenarian Prophet* (Minneapolis: Fortress, 1998); *The Historical Jesus and the Theological Jesus* (Grand Rapids, MI: Eerdmans, 2009); *Constructing Jesus* (Grand Rapids, MI: Baker Academic, 2010).

23. Norman Perrin, *The New Testament: An Introduction* (New York: Harcourt, Brace, Jovanovich, 1974). This is the first edition.

24. Burton L. Mack, *The Lost Gospel: The Book of Q and Christian Origins* (San Francisco: Harper, 1993).

25. J. D. Crossan, *The Historical Jesus: The Life of a Mediterranean Jewish Peasant* (San Francisco: Harper, 1991).

26. Harry T. Fleddermann, *Q: A Reconstruction and Commentary* (Leuven: Peeters, 1995). In the same year he produced a study of the overlaps (*Mark and Q* [BETL 122; Leuven: Peeters, 1995]) that includes a response by Neirynck.

27. D. Marguerat, "Pourquoi s'interesser a la Source?" in Andreas Dettwiler and Daniel Marguerat, ed., *La Source des Paroles de Jesus* (Geneva: Labor et Fides, 2008), 36–38.

28. Ulrich Luz, "Le regard de Matthieu sur la source," in Dettwiler and Marguerat, 271. Also F. Neirynck's assessment of Fleddermann's book, *Mark and Q* (BETL 122; Leuven: Peeters, 1995), 261–307.

29. *La source des paroles de Jesus (Q), aux origines du christianisme*, ed. Andreas Dettwiler and Daniel Marguerat (Geneva: Labor et Fides, 2008).

30. James D. G. Dunn, *A New Perspective on Jesus* (Grand Rapids, MI: Baker, 2005), 26–27, 40. Reply by Birger Gerhardsson, "The Secret of the Transmission of the Unwritten Jesus Tradition," *NTS* 51 (2005): 1–18; cf. Alan Kirk, "Orality, Writing, and Phantom Sources," *NTS* 58 (2012): 1–22.

31. G. B. Bazzana, "*Basileia* and Debt Relief: The Forgiveness of Debts in the Lord's Prayer in the Light of Documentary Papyri," *CBQ* 73 (2011): 511–25. This is only the first of several papers he is in the process of publishing at this time.

32. Benedict Thomas Viviano, "Who Wrote Q? The Sayings Document (Q) as the Apostle Matthew's Private Notebook as a Bilingual Village Scribe (Mark 2:13–17; Matt 9:9–13)," in *Mark and Matthew II*, ed. Eve-Marie Becker and Anders Runesson (WUNT 2.304; Tübingen: Mohr Siebeck, 2013), 75–91.

SELECT BIBLIOGRAPHY

I. Editions of Q

Amsler, Frederic. *L'evangile inconnu: La Source des paroles de Jesus*. Geneva: Labor et Fides, 2001.

Havener, Ivan, and Athanasius Polag. *Q: The Sayings of Jesus*. Wilmington, DE: Michael Glazier, 1987.

Hoffmann, Paul, and Christoph Heil. *Die Spruchquelle Q: Studienausgabe Griechisch und Deutsch*. Darmstadt, Germany: Wissenschaftliche Buchgesellschaft / Leuven: Peeters, 2002; 3rd ed., 2009.

Robinson, James M. *The Sayings of Jesus: The Sayings Gospel Q in English*. Minneapolis: Fortress, 2002.

Robinson, James M., Paul Hoffmann, and John S. Kloppenborg. *The Critical Edition of Q*. Minneapolis: Fortress / Leuven: Peeters, 2000.

II. Commentaries on Q

Fleddermann, H. T. *Q: A Reconstruction and Commentary*. Leuven: Peeters, 1995.

Manson, T. W. *The Sayings of Jesus*. London: SCM, 1937; Grand Rapids, MI: Eerdmans, 1979.

III. Studies on Q

Allison, Dale C. *The Intertextual Jesus: Scripture in Q.* Harrisburg, PA: Trinity Press International, 2000.

————. *The Jesus Tradition in Q.* Harrisburg, PA: Trinity Press International, 1997.

Boring, M. Eugene. *Sayings of the Risen Jesus: Christian Prophecy in the Synoptic Tradition.* SNTSMS 46; Cambridge: Cambridge University Press, 1982.

Burkitt, Francis Crawford. *The Gospel History and Its Transmission.* Edinburgh: T & T Clark, 1906.

Catchpole, David R. *The Quest for Q.* Edinburgh: T & T Clark, 1993.

Crossan, John Dominic. *In Fragments: The Aphorisms of Jesus.* San Francisco: Harper & Row, 1983.

Delobel, Joel, ed. Logia: *Les paroles de Jesus—The Sayings of Jesus: Memorial Joseph Coppens.* BETL 59; Louvain: Peeters, 1982.

Dettwiler, Andreas, and Daniel Marguerat, eds. *La source des paroles de Jesus (Q): Aux origines du christianisme.* Geneva: Labor et Fides, 2008.

Downing, F. G. "A Paradigm Perplex: Luke, Matthew and Mark." *NTS* 38 (1992): 15–36.

Dupont, Jacques. *Etudes sur les evangiles synoptiques.* 2 vols. BETL 70A-B; Leuven: Peeters, 1985.

Edwards, Richard A. *A Theology of Q: Eschatology, Prophecy, and Wisdom.* Philadelphia: Fortress, 1976.

————. *The Sign of Jonah in the Theology of the Evangelists and Q.* SBT 2/18; London: SCM, 1971.

Farrer, Austin M. "On Dispensing with Q." In *Studies in the Gospels in Memory of R. H. Lightfoot,* ed. Dennis E. Nineham. Oxford: Basil Blackwell, 1955.

Fleddermann, H. T. *Mark and Q: A Study of the Overlap Texts.* BETL 122; Leuven: Peeters, 1995.

Freyne, Sean. *Jesus, a Jewish Galilean: A New Reading of the Jesus Story.* Edinburgh: T & T Clark, 2005.

Goodacre, Mark S. *The Case Against Q: Studies in Markan Priority and the Synoptic Problem.* Harrisburg, PA: Trinity Press International, 2002.

Goodacre, Mark S., and Nicolas Perrin, ed. *Questioning Q: A Collection of Essays*. London: SPCK, 2004.

Goulder, Michael D. "Is Q a Juggernaut?" *JBL* 115 (1996): 667–81.

————. *Luke: A New Paradigm*. 2 vols. JSNTSup 20; Sheffield: JSOT Press, 1989.

————. "On Putting Q to the Test." *NTS* 24 (1978): 218–34.

————. *Midrash and Lection in Matthew*. London: SPCK, 1974.

Harnack, Adolf von. *The Sayings of Jesus: The Second Source of St. Matthew and St. Luke*. London: Williams and Norgate, 1907.

Head, Peter M. *Christology and the Synoptic Problem*. SNTSMS 94; Cambridge: University Press, 1997.

Hengel, Martin. *The Four Gospels and the One Gospel of Jesus Christ*. Harrisburg, PA: Trinity Press International, 2000.

Hoffmann, Paul. *Jesus von Nazareth und die Kirche: Spurensicherung im Neuen Testament*. Stuttgart: Verlag Katholisches Bibelwerk, 2009.

————. *Studien zur Theologie der Logienquelle*. NTAbh NF 8; Münster: Aschendorff, 1972.

Jacobson, Arland D. *The First Gospel: An Introduction to Q*. Sonoma, CA: Polebridge, 1992.

Kirk, Alan. *The Composition of the Sayings Source: Genre, Synchrony, and Wisdom Redaction in Q*. NovT Sup 91; Leiden: E. J. Brill, 1998.

Kloppenborg, J. S. *Q, the Earliest Gospel: An Introduction to the Original Stories and Sayings of Jesus*. Louisville, KY: Westminster John Knox, 2008.

————. *Excavating Q: The History and Setting of the Sayings Gospel*. Minneapolis: Fortress, 2000.

————. *The Formation of Q: Trajectories in Ancient Wisdom Collections*. Philadelphia: Fortress, 1987.

————, ed. *The Shape of Q: Signal Essays on the Sayings Gospel*. Minneapolis: Fortress, 1994.

Koester, Helmut, James M. Robinson. *Trajectories through Early Christianity*. Philadelphia: Fortress, 1971.

Levie, Jean, SJ. *The Bible: Word of God in Words of Men*. New York: P. J. Kennedy, 1961.

Lindemann, Andreas, ed. *The Sayings Source Q and the Historical Jesus*. BETL 158; Leuven: Peeters, 2001.

Mack, Burton Lee. *The Lost Gospel: The Book of Q and Christian Origins*. San Francisco: Harper, 1993.

Meier, John P. *A Marginal Jew: Rethinking the Historical Jesus. Vol. 2: Mentor, Message, and Miracles.* Anchor Yale Bible Reference Library. New York: Doubleday, 1994.

Montagnes, Bernard. *The Story of Father Marie-Joseph Lagrange, Founder of Modern Catholic Bible Study.* Translated by B. T. Viviano. New York / Mahwah, NJ: Paulist, 2006.

Neirynck, Frans, J. Verheyden , and R. Corstjens. *The Gospel of Matthew and the Gospel Source Q: A Cumulative Bibliography, 1950–1995.* 2 vols. BETL 140a; Leuven: Peeters, 1998.

Piper, Ronald A. *Wisdom in the Q Tradition: The Aphoristic Teaching of Jesus.* SNTSMS 61: Cambridge: University Press, 1989.

Polag, Athanasius. "The Theological Center of the Sayings Source." In *The Gospel and the Gospels*, ed. Peter Stuhlmacher, 97–105. Grand Rapids, MI: Eerdmans, 1991.

Robinson, James M. *The Gospel of Jesus: In Search of the Original Good News.* San Francisco: Harper, 2005.

Schillebeeckx, Edward. *Jesus: An Experiment in Christology.* New York: Seabury, 1979.

Schmid, Josef. *Matthaeus und Lukas: Eine Untersuchung des Verhaeltnisses ihrer Evangelien.* Freiburg: Herder, 1930.

Schottroff, Luise, and Wolfgang Stegemann. *Jesus and the Hope of the Poor.* Maryknoll, NY: Orbis, 1986.

Solages, Bruno de. *Comment sont nes les evangiles Marc, Luc, Matthieu.* Paris: Editions ouvrieres, 1973.

Streeter, B. H. *The Four Gospels: A Study of Origins, Treating of the Manuscript Tradition, Sources, Authorship, & Dates.* London: Macmillan, 1924.

Todt, Heinz Eduard. *The Son of Man in the Synoptic Tradition.* London: SCM, 1965.

Tuckett, Christopher M. *Q and the History of Early Christianity: Studies on Q.* Edinburgh: T & T Clark, 1996.

———. "On the Relationship between Matthew and Luke." *NTS* 30 (1984): 130–42.

Vaage, Lief. *Galilean Upstarts: Jesus' First Followers According to Q.* Valley Forge, PA: Trinity Press International, 1994.

Van Segbroeck, Frans, C. M. Tuckett, G. Van Belle, and Joseph Verheyden, eds. *The Four Gospels 1992: Festschrift Frans Neirynck.* 3 vols. BETL 100; Leuven: Peeters, 1992.

Vassiliades, Petros. "The Nature and Extent of the Q Document." *NovT* 20 (1978): 49–73.

Watson, Francis. "Q as Hypothesis." *NTS* 55 (2009): 397–415.

Wikenhauser, Alfred. *New Testament Introduction.* New York: Herder & Herder, 1958.

Zeller, Dieter. *Kommentar zur Logienquelle.* Stuttgarter Kleiner Kommentar Neues Testament 21; Stuttgart: Katholisches Bibelwerk, 1993.

———. "Exegese als Anstoss fuer systematische Eschatologie." In P. Fiedler, D. Zeller, eds., *Gegenwart und kommendes Reich.* Stuttgart: Katholisches Bibelwerk, 1975.

INDEX OF NAMES

INDEX OF SCRIPTURE, Q, AND ANCIENT TEXTS